OTHER BOOKS BY JERRY VASS

• MECHANICS OF SELLING

• SOFT SELLING IN A HARD WORLD

• SELLING IN AMERICA

• SLEEPING BIG IN SMALLVILLE

SOFT SELLING TO EXECUTIVES

Jerry Vass
and
Iris Herrin

Previously titled:
Decoding the BS of Business
© 2006, 2016 VASS Publishing

ISBN-13: 978-0-9629610-7-6
ISBN-10: 0-9629610-7-8

Previously titled:
Decoding the BS of Business

VASS Publishing
1093 A1A Beach Boulevard Suite 448
Saint Augustine, FL 32080
904-461-0452

This book may be ordered from www.amazon.com

*"The beginning of wisdom is calling
things by their right name."*

- Chinese Proverb

Table of Contents

Foreword

Executives and professionals speak different languages, as disparate as Swahili and Greek. Agendas, vocabularies, and cultural conditioning destroy meaningful communication between them.

This book exposes selling myths and profit-killing gaps between illusion and reality.

Executives live in a different world than the rest of us. They think differently, act differently, and buy differently. For the professions—those in our culture who package and sell information for a living—architects, lawyers, engineers, accountants, brokers, MBAs, CPAs, marketers, and consultants of every stripe, persuasion and profession, a shift of thinking is required to design and hold a Persuasive Executive Conversation.

A number of preconceptions and cultural myths need to be bulldozed to clear the way for this thinking shift. Three things are required to answer the Buyer's questions and sell well in the executive suite: the story, the tools, and the delivery. We will explore each and help you prepare a presentation that works from the executive's point of view, that you can take into any boardroom, tell your story, and double your chances of getting hired.

When selling to executives *what* you sell is different from *how* you sell it. While professionals are expert at delivering services to their clients, they are amateurs at telling people what they do for a living. These skills are not taught at Harvard, Yale, or State U.

Our job is to help people make money. For nearly three decades we have intensively trained 12,000 managers, professional salespeople, and consultants to persuade at the executive level. While doing so, we discovered a critical element that managers overlook or ignore that can cost one-quarter of sales revenues or more.

So what is this low-grade infection that limits a firm's potential and costs so much money? What is this counter intuitive malaise that works against the philosophies and strategies of reputable companies managed by bright, educated people? It is this: corporations and consulting firms spend big money to hide what they do from their Buyers.*

It is nearly impossible to get a company, much less a salesperson, to explain what they do for a living stated in Buyer's terms; they cannot tell a selling story that is different from the competitors', makes sense in the Buyer's world, or is even interesting. In many cases, they insult the Buyer's intelligence. It is called business bullshit, and henceforth we refer to it in less scatological terms. But there are times in life when one must call something by its right name.

What we learned from our Clients will surprise you as it did us: If a firm can cut the BS and answer five logical questions on the mind of every executive-level Buyer, sales successes can double.

*For simplicity, we use "Buyer" throughout this text as the person or group who makes the buying decision and will at some point buy from someone if not you.

We use "Client" as a person or company who has already bought your services.

"Seller" is the person or firm who must gain commitment from a Buyer.

The generic terms "manager" and "management" identify those responsible and accountable for their firm's direction, including money-making or -losing decisions.

Every anecdote is true but sometimes names have been changed for obvious reasons.

Missing the Point

Words mean different things to the Buyer and Seller. You'll find these missed communications are more than just disagreements or misunderstandings about syntax, idiom, and vernacular but go to the underlying mechanics of persuasive communication. This book is about the translations required to communicate with the executive-level Buyer.

You may be surprised, as we were, to find that common cultural illusions and business myths restrict business growth as surely as shortage of capital, lack of innovation, or outdated ideas.

We have identified sixteen myths that erode profits based on information and observations developed from our ten-year study of 3,424 salespeople, heavily weighted towards those with professional degrees, high skill levels, and street experience. As observers and teachers, we identified some of the problems that hobble sales messages. The VASS® Study (Appendix A) is the result; the statistics we quote are derived from that study. With the help of Reality Checks, a tape recorder, and a two-dollar calculator you may develop your own study of the people responsible for producing your firm's revenues.

Reality Checks

You may enjoy testing your own organization and its people to discover how Buyers view your business and why your people are hard to buy from. You may find that things you thought were important to the Buyer aren't. And that the things you ignored are vital. You may discover how comfortably your people rest in the warm embrace of conventional wisdom and that what your people actually do and say in high-level presentations are not what the executive buyer wants. Once you see the problems, you can avoid them, learn to respect your Buyer's intelligence, and capture revenues that would otherwise go undiscovered. The VASS® Study, along with your own eyes and ears, will confirm your observations.

Chapter 1—The Ugly Baby

Confession of a Slow Thinker

It took us 20 years for us to catch on to this expensive problem.

As sales trainers we always worked with the underlying assumption that our clients had good stuff to sell with good stories to tell about it. After all, they were big companies with unlimited resources, had framed degrees hung on their paneled walls, spent millions on advertising and marketing, and gave away tickets to high-end sporting events.

Our job is to enter the training room with a naïve mind, that is, the "Buyer's mind," and help participants translate their expertise into a story for their Buyer, format the presentation mechanics, and formulate the delivery of their new value position. We act as their Buyer while avoiding their whirlpool of endless discussions about internal corporate problems. Their stories, however, never seemed connected to the Buyer; they seemed flawed in some indefinable way; many times, things we knew to be true sounded untrue when listened to with the Buyer's ear.

A Flawed Delivery

After hearing hundreds of selling stories, suspicion dawned slowly; it crept into our consciousness as a shadow rather than arriving with trumpets. One misty morning the gauzy, wafting, underlying suspicion turned solid; shaped itself into a hard, unpleasant truth: it was an ugly baby; the realization that salespeople, their managers, marketers, and their companies have no story to tell from the Buyer's point of view. While the Seller's message about themselves, their credentials, and processes sounds good in their own ears, the business proposition they offer makes little sense from the Buyer's side. The reason? The Seller's real objective is to create a story that glorifies the corporate ego rather than speak to the Buyer. While the professional is delivering his shtick about the "Glories of Us," his Buyers look and listen in vain for "How do these people fit into my business? What does this mean for me?"

The ugly and expensive baby is the failure to communicate in the Buyer's terms.

The Executive's Big Five

In sales presentations, both in person and in print, Sellers should be able to handily answer the five simple questions on every executive Buyer's mind (all buyers for that matter):

- Why should I spend my time talking to you?

- Why should I buy from you rather than your competitor?

- What makes you different from them?

- Why should I pay you more when they charge less?

- Why should I switch from the service provider I know?

At first glance, the usual and predictable reaction of both salespeople and their managers is "Of course, we can answer these questions. We do it every day."

It is true they answer questions every day but not these questions. Everyone we meet can tell us what he does technically: his expertise, his history, his processes, and his philosophy. But seldom is one of the executive's five questions answered.

The Story

We use the word "story" throughout this book. For clarity here is what we mean: "Story"—from the Latin *historia*—means a narrative, an account, or description.

The **Seller's story** we speak of is the narrative about his own processes, procedures, point of view, philosophy, features, and advantages of his business—his "stuff"—usually delivered in the form of an overlong and complicated pitch. The more sophisticated call it a presentation.

The **Buyer's story** we discuss is the translation of the Seller's story into the Buyer's language and interest; it is a truthful, provable narrative delivered in the Buyer's language; it is the underlying information, benefits, and value position that creates an executive-level dialogue. It is usually delivered in the form of a Persuasive Executive Conversation that answers the Buyer's five questions. It is not a pitch—it is a civilized dialog.

Don't be fooled: It is a complex challenge to change sides, to put yourself in the executive buyer's shoes; to think like he does.

A meeting with the CEO averages fifteen minutes. Persuasion at the boardroom level must be done simply, quickly, quantifiably, and provably. There is no time for close analysis of the Buyer's personality type or intricate technical discussions about "how we do it."

Our ten-year study showed us that of all the firms we have taught (big ones and little, products and services), none have been able to answer the executive's five questions.

Every day in our business, we watch the best lose simply because management and salespeople act and talk the opposite of their intentions; their execution isn't congruent with their objectives.

This is a story about beautiful parents giving birth to ugly babies who are embarrassing to take out of the house. The good news: Once you understand what a pretty baby looks like, you can create one of your own.

CHAPTER 2—THREE SINS

A Business Miracle

The Brits hurried along in the lowering weather as if each had a hotel tryst with a secret lover.

The early-morning traffic on London's Strand was chockablock. A taxicab with a large and stylish advertising logo painted on the door slid up to the curb; the slogan beneath the logo promised a business miracle: "Differentbiz.com—Transforming Business."[1]

Forty-five years in business have taught me that transforming business is what each manager must do: invent, reinvent, find, and fill ever-changing and more demanding markets; control the thousands of variables that over time, willingly or not, painfully transform every business that survives the rough-and-tumble of capitalism. Now here, advertising on a cab door, was an organization that could help avoid the pain that constant change entails.

As I was invited to do, I visited the company on the Internet and sent this email:

> Dear Sir:
>
> I saw your ad on a taxi and visited your web site. Your business name and slogan,

differentbiz.com— "Transforming Business," implies you have some business magic.

My question is, in plain English, what do you do for a living? Contrary to the implication in your name, your web site looks like every other site. What do you sell? What specific business problems do you solve? What history do you have with your Buyers? What is your business objective from your Buyer's point of view?

The answer I got back was typically British in tone—courteous and solicitous, certainly more pleasant than the abrasive American tone of my email:

Mr. Vass,

Thank you for your recent enquiry. It was both direct and refreshing in its line of questioning.

We are a management consulting firm assisting companies in the process of transforming their existing business endeavours into future market strategies. We accomplish this by ensuring a company is managed effectively. Further, we suggest action for improvement, creating true value and allowing companies to compete more effectively, thus stimulating growth in today's somewhat chaotic environment.

Our education and experience place us in a uniquely qualified position to provide a vast scope of valuable services to our buyers, allowing them to achieve the results they seek.

Whilst we cannot, of course, disclose our client list, we can confirm that due to our broad range of professional consulting skills our clients have proven to be entirely satisfied with our services.We are most grateful for your enquiry. If there is anything further we can do for you, please contact us by telephone.

Yours sincerely, Nigel Farthing, Ph.D., MA (Oxon.)

Chairman

It was a crystallizing moment when I realized that the simplest questions from a potential Buyer (me) could not be answered by a firm promising to "transform my business." This reply was an "Aren't we smart" sales message from a firm promising not just to help but to *transform*.

This gulf between a firm and its potential buyers is caused by three sins: myth, conventional wisdom, and institutional arrogance.

Mythology

Selling myths—popular beliefs and traditions—cause Sellers to blindly pass their Buyers like ships in the night.

If you are in sales, marketing, or management, swim out into deeper water with us and judge for yourself. There is nothing mystical here. Everything in this book is self-evident once you see it.

The most expensive business myth is that one pitch fits all. Traditional selling, based in myth and developed for low-level sales presentations, is the very thing that will get a salesperson politely but firmly escorted off the executive floor.

Conventional Wisdom

The late John Kenneth Galbraith is credited with inventing the term "conventional wisdom," which he defined as simple, convenient, comfortable, and comforting but not necessarily true.

The most common reaction we hear from managers is, "Conventional wisdom is not our problem. That doesn't apply to my company or my people. We are creative; we are different."

Conventional wisdom does apply to you. If you were raised in America you were encultured by television, McDonald's, the NFL, Nike, and

Pillsbury. You have been imprinted by college profs, ad agencies, and talking heads; bombarded by billboards, bold headlines and sexy images. Conventional wisdom is like gravity: It can't be denied. It relentlessly pulls us into its vortex and makes us do silly, counterproductive things. You couldn't and didn't resist. None of us did.

Institutional Arrogance

Institutional arrogance is basing decisions on "What's good for us" vs. "What's good for our Buyers." It is the pervasive feeling inside the firm that the Seller is smarter than the Buyer, who "just doesn't get it."

This superior feeling is a compulsive rodent gnawing at the guts of business. Once alerted, you see it everywhere. The garden for institutional arrogance is seeded as soon as three people come together to grow a business. Turning inward, working on *our stuff* and *our version of the truth* can be as fulfilling as doing business with customers, perhaps more so. But this inward focus can kill your business while still a seedling.

Institutional arrogance isn't a capital crime but it annoys Buyers and blinds your own people to the realities of competition. It helps your salespeople deny that the competition is very smart and very good. Like professional athletes, each person on the playing field can win on any given day, and the differences among competitors, in absolute terms, is small, perhaps thousandths of a second.

On the business playing field, the actual differences may be only slightly larger. The differences can be increased exponentially, however, by changing the Buyer's perception of your firm. Becoming unique in the Buyer's eyes demands a Persuasive Executive Conversation.

• •

IBM suffered a near-death experience from institutional arrogance.

IBMers, once known as the best salespeople in the world, became mediocre candidates in the job market.

Who would have believed that such bright, talented people could fall from such a high place? How did this disaster come to be? Actually it was rather simple—the company turned inward.

"Doing business" the IBMers called it. That was where Department A did business with Department B, which in turn worked for Departments C, D, and A, completing the circle entirely within the walls of the company. IBM became a cult; it developed a belief system and a private internal language. Outsiders—customers, vendors, and other interlopers—were an inconvenience and barely tolerated.

When the customer managed to burgle his way into the "doing business" circle, he discovered that IBM specialized in studies, needs assessments, and inventories rather than sales and service.

An IBM rep said, "If a customer says to us, 'I need a workstation on that desk over there,' we say we'll come back on Monday and study the problem.

"Conversely, our competitor will pull a workstation out of his car trunk and install it on the spot."

"The best sales force in the world" became design-oriented techies burdened by technical knowledge carefully taught to them by IBM sales school, which was actually a product familiarization school. Even innate persuasion skills drowned in a sea of equipment features continually being pumped out by the largest anti-sales computer company in the world.

IBM engineers assumed that if they designed computers, no matter how unfriendly, the buyer would be forced to use them regardless of the user's agony or expense. Apple designers seemed to understand intuitively that the easier the computer was to use, the more use it would get. So they introduced the intuitive, point-and-click environment (actually invented by Xerox) that made Macintoshes simple to operate.

With their engineer-driven logic and we-only-talk-to-ourselves operating style, IBM inadvertently opened the door for Apple Computer and lost its unique place in the personal computer marketplace the day the Macintosh was conceived.

Had IBM truly been 100% customer-driven, as it avowed it was, it would have designed its products for ease of operation. And the nerds in the garage that kluged together the Macintosh for us computer-ignorant people would have instead started a garage band.

• •

During the birth of a business, many times the Buyer is demoted to a gray, faceless "them" loitering outside the circle of "our" bright light of creativity. In the heat and excitement of building a business, it is easy to forget that the Buyer is an integral part of it, more important to the business model and its success than the chairman of the board, venture capitalist, or the senior partner.

This confusion between "us" and "them" can be infinitely subtle. My team once spent three years designing an interactive software program that taught people how to build a selling presentation from the Buyer's point of view.

As we progressed with the writing and designing, the program worked better and better. Needless to say, I was stoked on this terrific product and the benefits it could deliver to the small business owner.

But I had trouble selling the idea to my friends. They asked me, "Why will people buy this?"

I could never convince them that people would actually spend the money. I plunged ever deeper into the American Dream, confident that when the program was completed, when people saw it in its singular splendor, they would declare it, like Edison's light bulb, the work of genius and buy like crazy. It would sell itself.

I ignored the doubters. After all, Babe Ruth struck out 1,330 times, so quitting was not an option. Even my programmer, who was well supported by this project, couldn't get it. Once a month he would look sideways at me and say, "I think this program is brilliant. I just don't understand how you're gonna sell it."

My reply was always the same: "Just don't worry your pretty little ponytail about it. You do the programming. I'll do the selling. That's what I do for a living. Now, let's talk about some improvements I thought up last night." And so it went for three years: improvements, changes, upgrades, rewrites, new approaches, new ideas, new brilliance always in the works.

Then we went to market and found that, indeed, every one of my critics was right and I was wrong. There was no market. I had designed a solution for a problem Buyers did not know they had. (And if they didn't know they had it, then they probably didn't.)

I didn't listen to my potential customers when they told me they already knew how to sell, how to present, how to persuade. I knew from my years of training that they didn't know and that they left half of their revenues on the table. So I became intent on making them learn my stuff. While I was aware of my Buyers, I was much more involved in the design of my brainstorm, my baby, my genius, my imagined fame and wealth. And I failed because I forgot that the Buyer had to fully participate in my idea. I had given birth to an ugly baby.

Now failure is not death but it can be discouraging. Even so, I was not terribly distraught about the failure of the idea. Or, about the money wasted never to be recovered. The most discouraging element was the nine man-years wasted on an idea that would have died at birth if I had not wrapped myself in the flag of personal arrogance and defended my idea against my own market. I should have listened to them more and held fewer pillow-talk discussions with my navel. I exploded my own dot-bomb several years before the Silicon Valley bubble burst.

• •

Reality Check: Institutional Arrogance

Institutional arrogance is a costly disease. How do you tell if your people are infected? Ask yourself these questions. (In every reality check, we suggest you record your people's answers. Many times they will deny saying things and a recording will settle arguments. Prepare for lots of squirming when your people hear what they actually say.)

- Is your stuff and your story built for you or for your Buyers?

- Are your firm's decisions based on what's good for you or what's good for your Buyers?

- Do you spend more time discussing your company and product or service issues than you do customer issues?

- Do you consider internal politics and functions "doing business"?

- Are in-house "clients" (co-workers) as important as outside paying clients?

- Do you watch the competition rather than the Buyer? (Anxiety about competitors takes your eye off the Buyer's needs.)

- Have you evolved a private language? Inward-looking organizations love their own jargon.

The bigger the organization, the more likely the language is to develop into parochial mysticism. In some firms the jargon becomes so obscure that even the insiders can't explain what it means.

- Do you speak of customers in a disparaging way?

- Do you do "All about us!" show-and-tell presentations? They are a sure sign your firm has turned inward on itself.

- Do clients with problems get bounced around inside the firm?

- Do your hear comments like:

  Our Buyers can't live without us.

  Our services sell themselves.

  We have a feature nobody else has.

  We are much better than our competition.

  Our Buyers just don't get it.

  Some people aren't smart enough to hire us.

- Or, if a sale doesn't close,

  That Buyer isn't playing with a full deck.

- Which come from attitudes like

  We're right and everybody else is wrong.

  We have the highest quality stuff in our industry.

  We are the best and nobody else is in our league.

  We should get the business just because we are so good.

  We are the smartest people in our industry.

  Our buyers are not smart enough to understand how good we are.

  Anyone who doesn't hire us is a loser.

Once upon a time we were invited to present at an annual meeting of senior consultants. We had a long and successful history with these folks and helped them make a lot of money. We were the only outsiders invited, mostly to observe and then give a short, upbeat program.

The managing partner of the firm gave a keynote speech to a big room filled with his people. Not once did he mention their clients or the clients' irreplaceable role in their business.

Over the next day talented experts huddled on the spacious lawns of the luxury seaside hotel and swapped stories. In one conversation I overheard the question from one senior partner to another, "How much money did we take off those people?"

As these dismissive and disparaging attitudes about the clients became more and more obvious, I became more and more angry (read crazy). We had been teaching these same folk to become 100% client-conscious and they were talking like their firm was a self-supporting organization where clients were an intrusion into their self-satisfied little world.

I spent a sleepless night. During those long hours I became convinced they were committing business suicide.

The next morning, during my talk to them, I got a testosterone rush and lost my place in the universe; became arrogant; and gave them a round, sound, military-style ass chewing.

I lost touch with my client. I got fired.

• •

Chapter 3—Say What?

Feature / Advantage / Benefit

You are driving down the freeway and you pass a truck with lettering that says, "Bob's Racing Shop—We Make Cars Go Real Fast." Is there any doubt about what business Bob is in?

You are passed by another truck: "Nash's Tree Nursery—Instant Shade for Rich People." Another clean communication.

You go by a billboard and a law firm announces "Represent the injured. That's what we do." Got it.[2]

A mile farther on you pass a truck that says, "Lucent Technology—Bell Labs Innovations." What business is this company in? What does it do?

Curious, you go to the web site and click open the company's home page. It doesn't explain anything either; not even a hint. What is the problem with this company? Why can't it tell us what it does for a living? What's the big secret?

Marketers approach their story in a predictable way: features of the services, their stuff, and their processes. Because they can't (or won't) explain what their firm does in simple words, they resort to high-sounding slogans like:

- Navigating a New World

- From Thought to Finish

- Innovative Thinking

- Transforming Business

- How Business Gets Done

- The Power to Simplify

Slogans are created at great expense by marketing departments and advertising agencies. Assume now that you are a buyer of services. Which of these slogans do you believe is true? Which one gives you the sense of trust you need to separate you from your money?

A comparable and equally pithy slogan might be "The Tooth Fairy is Your Rich Friend."

When it comes to selling, managers are burdened by three fraudulent assumptions:

1. Everybody cares about our stuff.

2. If Buyers know the technical information we know, they will see how good we are.

3. Buyers believe us because we are DifferentBiz, Inc., a global company that specializes in everything for everybody, 24/7/365.

The ugly baby reality is this:

1. Nobody cares about who you are, what you have to sell, or what you say. Nobody hears you when you glorify yourself.

2. Nobody cares about your stuff. Buyers care only if your stuff is a means to their end, that is, the results your service brings to the Buyer in *his* context. Buyers don't want to know the technical information you know. If they did, they would be in your business, most likely as your competitor.

3. Buyers do not confuse institutional arrogance with corporate truthfulness. More and more, Buyers are feeling the gap between what service providers say and how they act—that companies are too big, don't listen, don't respond, tell lies, and cheat whenever possible.

What Buyers are looking for:

- candor and solutions to their business problems

- a solution that fits the problem as described by performance, function, and core benefits at a fair price

- your business to be honest, accountable, consistent, reliable

On the other hand, Buyers:

- distrust your business motives and integrity

- reject puffery—they regard hype and omission as lies[3]

EXECUTIVE SELLING

is explaining well what you do from
the Buyer's point of view.

Reality Check: Your Business Story

"You can observe a lot just by watchin'."

—Yogi Berra

Selling well isn't trickery or a war of wits—it's skillful and truthful storytelling. Tricks may temporarily carry the day but over the long haul, you will be found out and pushed away by cynical Buyers. Selling is about trust—building it, maintaining it, protecting it. You can't maintain trust with trickery.

You'll find your salespeople, even the cockiest of your group, are 99% predictable; your Buyer sees it every day and is bored stiff. (It is one reason appointments with upper management are so hard to get.)

Here is a question you can ask your top guns to see if your intended message is decoded for the Buyer. (Don't be shy: pick the best you have. Their predicted responses are in italics. Remember to record this exercise.)

Have them present a 60-second commercial about your services.

(This will be a rambling, stumbling, all-feature presentation about the glories of the firm, the stuff, and the presenter personally. The word "I" will figure prominently in the pitch. There will be little if anything about the Buyer's problems or benefits for the Buyer. Provable numbers or business context will rarely be mentioned. If ever. In street parlance this performance is called a pitch.)

Buyers hate to be pitched. They love civilized conversation; they want you to engage them. The executive buyer doesn't care about the glories of your firm or the salesperson, only about what is in it for him: increased sales, decreased costs, increased image, higher profits, cash flow, return on investment, reduced risk, etc.

Chapter 4—Circles of Confusion

The Seller's failure to communicate with the Buyer is caused by the confusion between puffery and representation. More confusion is stirred in when the Seller does not understand the differences between features, advantages, and benefits.

Let's make this clear: The firms we reference here are terrific at what they do. They are the leaders in their field, are award winners, and work at the highest levels of business. There is nothing in this book that implies they are anything less than superstars when it comes to their actual performance for their clients.

We chose our examples arbitrarily. Simply touring around the Internet yielded hundreds of examples that reveal the gap between the great services firms provide and the "ugly baby" stories they tell their potential buyers.

Beautiful Parents—Ugly Baby

Our first example was ranked number one by both the *Financial Times* and "Business Week". (While our examples may not be from your specific profession, they are typical of all the professions.)

This beautiful parent is Duke Corporate Education, a for-profit corporation held by Duke University. They draw on 1,000 experts from 25 countries to deliver $40 million in consulting services across six continents to clients like IBM, PricewaterhouseCoopers, Lehman Brothers, Honeywell, and Microsoft. Obviously these are smart people who know what they are doing.

This is a direct quote from its web site (http://www.dukece.com/) headlined **Benefits to Clients.**[+] (We have italicized some of their content to make a point later.):

Education in Business Context.

We help our clients implement their strategy through development of their people. We focus education on what the organization's people need to know, do and believe in order to address current or anticipated challenges, and attain specific business objectives. We refer to that as strategy execution through education.

Education creates the capability *to move the organization forward now and in the future.*

Education can:

- Enable the creation of the organization's strategy

- Guide the articulation, translation and understanding of the strategy and business imperatives by the people who have to execute

- Build the organizational capabilities needed to implement it

- Shape the behaviors, beliefs and values needed *to get it done right*

Our goal is to develop individual competencies within the broader framework of developing the organization's capability to address its business challenges. *It is our point of view that for the CLO, education focused on organizational capabilities is a powerful business lever to make strategy happen;* and for the CLO, developing organizational capabilities *increases the impact of the education.*

That linkage of education to strategy is not an all-or-none notion; it is a continuum. At one end is the individual competency development. At the other end is individual competency development within the context of organizational competency development. A middle ground is competency development informed by the firm's strategic context.

Duke CE programs fall through the range depending on the buyer's needs.

Definitions

Individual competency: an individual's leadership or functional ability; his or her ability to *get work done.*

Organizational Capability

An organization's ability to execute strategic activities; its ability to address its business suppliers...

...To meet the broad range of needs our buyers bring to us we draw on quality faculty from numerous business schools. We also leverage non-faculty educators such as coaches, facilitators, industry experts, retired executives, actors and others committed to high-quality customized education.

The Vault (www.thevault.com) named the 50 most prestigious consulting firms. Here are web site samples from five of the top ten. To spice it up, we have added lawyers, architects, business strategists, engineers and commercial real estate brokers. Under the general heading of "what we do," here are some outtakes. Compare them.[5]

- Spanning almost 75 years, our history is rich with great clients and award-winning projects. But our future is even brighter. Armed with specialized expertise and a clear mission, our talented staff operates from strategically positioned offices to provide superior services. We are an organization that values achievement, prizes leadership, seeks innovation and rewards breakthrough thinking. (Walter P Moore)

- Marakon Associates is a leading strategy and management consulting firm, and the world's foremost authority on value creation.

- Local Real Estate, Worldwide—CB Richard Ellis is the global leader in real estate services.

- We identify creative and efficient solutions—for today and tomorrow. We live in a changing world—one that requires meeting challenges and identifying creative and efficient solutions on a daily basis and over time. Never before has the need to plan, budget, implement, and manage been more important. (Woolpert, Inc.)

- Mercer Oliver Wyman is a leader in financial services and risk management consulting. The firm has more than 900 staff working out of 27 offices in 13 countries throughout North America, Europe, and Asia Pacific.

- At Clough Harbour & Associates, our success comes as a direct result of a company culture that values outstanding client service above all else. Our commitment to setting a new standard of client service, coupled with our diverse offering of high-quality engineering and planning solutions, continues to turn new clients into lifelong advocates. We are proud to say that always giving our clients more than they expect has been the foundation of our success for over 50 years.

- The Boston Consulting Group is an international strategy and general management consulting firm whose mission is to help corporations create and sustain competitive advantage. As a truly international firm, our strong global presence offers clients and employees a wealth of cross-cultural experience.

- Our mission: to help our clients make distinctive, lasting, and substantial improvement in their performance to build a great firm that attracts, develops, excites, and retains exceptional people. (McKinsey & Company)

- O'Melveny & Myers LLP is guided by the principles of excellence, leadership, and citizenship. With the breadth, depth, and foresight to serve clients competing in a global economy, our lawyers devise innovative approaches to resolve problems and achieve business goals.

- As one of the world's premier corporate strategy and operations firms, Mercer Management Consulting helps leading enterprises develop, build, and operate strong businesses that deliver sustained shareholder value growth.

- Black & Veatch is Building a World of Difference by challenging the frontiers of knowledge to provide energy, water, information and other vital infrastructure for a better world. We lead our industry in value creation for each of our stakeholders -clients, professionals, shareholders and business partners.

- An experienced business advisor and systems integrator provides you with the right advice and solutions with your best interests in mind. BearingPoint's accelerated solutions combine our deep industry knowledge with technology expertise that brings real, tangible enterprise value to you.

- Baker & McKenzie is the world's leading global law firm. We have provided sophisticated legal advice and services to many of the world's most dynamic and global organizations for more than 50 years. With a network of more than 3,000 locally qualified, internationally

experienced lawyers in 38 countries, we
have the knowledge and resources to
deliver the broad scope of quality legal
services required for both international
and local clients - consistently, with
confidence and with sensitivity for
cultural, social and legal practice
differences.

Welcome to the world of conventional wisdom—
simple, convenient, comfortable, and comforting—
for the Sellers.

As we said before, these firms are superb at what
they do and the services they deliver set industry
standards. The question is: Do they tell a story
that differentiates them?

Circles Within Lies—Puffery

Webster's Dictionary defines **puffery** as "flattering publicity; exaggerated commendations especially for promotional purposes."

The U.S. Federal Trade Commission (FTC) says, "The term 'puffing' refers generally to an expression of opinion not made as a representation of fact that ordinary consumers do not take seriously; expressions of opinion not made as a representation of fact...subjective claims (taste, feel, appearance, smell) and hyperbole [that] are not capable of objective measurement [and are] subjective appeals at the expense of objective data... " (FTC 1984a)

"It implies that [the advertiser] does not have definite knowledge... [it is] the difference between 'This is true,' and 'I think this is true, but I am not sure...' buyers are expected to and do understand that they are not entitled to rely literally upon the words." [6]

Vagueness is a handy way to avoid responsibility for your Buyer's story if you do not know the quantifiable results of your processes. Of course, big, broad-ranging and generalized vagueness, "We can help," is better than specific vagueness. This is America. Even empty promises have the duty to be big.

Puffery is a waste of time and effort. It makes the salesperson look incompetent, amateurish and less than honest. It sets up conflicts with Buyers and creates lawsuits. Worst of all, it makes your presentation blend into the gray background of your competitors.

Here is some typical and easily recognizable puffery:

- Number 1
- The best
- The only
- More profits
- Save money
- A lot
- Highest quality
- Lowest cost
- Fastest
- Profitable

Puffery is subjective—the Seller's opinion. Market studies show that Buyers consider the Seller's opinions to be lies.

To paraphrase an expert, Dr. Ivan Preston, Journal Communications Professor Emeritus, University of Wisconsin–Madison, in the *Journal of Consumer Affairs*:

"[Puffery] is called anti-factual content because... rather then being informative, i.e., a true fact claim, about a product or service, it is either non-informative, providing no fact at all about the item, or mis-informative, providing a false fact about it [and]...may detract from information rather than add to it...[because]...puffery, the marketplace term for claims explicitly of opinion rather than fact...[is]...factually meaningless...[thus] meaning consumers see [puffery] as detracting from information."[7]

In the Duke example above, we have placed the obvious puffery in italics.

The chasm between Duke and its Buyers is created by purely subjective phrases like "...high quality customized education...." Such phrases are the Seller's opinion and, therefore, designed not to be taken seriously.

This advertising goes to great lengths to sound superior to both the reader and their potential Buyers. Only insiders can decipher what Duke is saying. But this much is certain: Virtually every word that isn't puffery is about features and advantages (the process) of Duke's services, which they never translate into the stunning results they deliver to their buyers. In short, it is both anti-factual and non-informative.

Word Fashion

Business buzzwords that fall in and out of fashion like women's clothes are almost always puffery. We call them "black hole" words because they absorb more energy from the transaction than they produce and each has several interpretations; thus are totally subjective.

- Relationship

- Value-added

- World class

- Professional

- Full service

- Innovative

- Ownership

- Dedicated

- Solutions

- Win-Win

- Creative

- Technical expertise

- Outside the box

- Sales training

- Best of breed

- Partnership

- Paradigm

- Scaleable

- Synergy

- Proactive

- Reliable

- Robust

- Profit

It is likely you have some black hole words to add from your own private collection. If you Google "bullshit bingo" you'll find many others.

You will notice that professionals, consultants, politicians, motivational speakers, and advertising agencies love black hole words; they think these words can't come back and bite them because these words have no teeth.

Not true. Hairy lawsuits with fangs spring from the pink, pillow-soft loins of puffery.

• •

Because they were unhappy with the services they were receiving, a client sued a now-defunct Big Eight firm for misrepresentation. In their sales proposal the firm said, "We are world class providers for [a specialized service]."

Later the Client discovered that the seller was not the "market leader" in that specialized service, hadn't "written the book" about it and their performance did not approach the Client's definition of "world class." The Client convinced the court that the consultant's sales puffery was actually professional misrepresentation.

The disgruntled Client won. The court nullified the contract, awarded damages and made the sellers disgorge their fee.

• •

One hundred percent of professionals use puffery, that is, unproven claims, until trained not to do so.

In Truth

"I respond to the persuasive power of a simple message that explains how you benefit me. But I think that you respond to reams of technical information, jargon, lies, obfuscation, and arrogance."

—Bubba Ram, Salesman

Representation is objective; an expression of facts, "… a positive assertion that the fact is true. It implies that the maker has definite knowledge or information which justifies the positive assertion."[8]

Here are some examples of representation:

- Improve profits 3%

- Decrease costs by 11%

- Increase fees by 22%

- 26 engineers

- All credentials, CPA, Ph.D., etc.

- Produce product twice as fast

- $200 an hour

- 3 times longer

- 220 employees

- 40% markup

- 12 years in business

- 2,410 installations
- 39 offices nationwide

Buyers want to hear representation, the truth, something real stated as provable facts. When a firm talks facts in the context of the Buyer's business life, avoiding loss or the prospect of gain (the only reasons people buy anything), the business story takes a dramatic turn. It becomes concrete and solid and believable in the form of return on investment (ROI), additional profits, reduced overhead, increased efficiency, employee morale, reduced insurance costs, etc. It differentiates one service provider or company from another. Suddenly, you sound honest. Honesty builds trust. Trust builds a steady and faithful clientele.

In our prior examples, even facts are all tarted up with puffery.

Puffery:

- makes your company, products, services, and your people look sleazy

- weakens your story

- dulls your competitive edge; makes you sound like everybody else

- reduces your price to the competitors'

- infects 100% of your company from top to bottom; everybody does it

Reality Check: Puffery

Using provable facts only—not puffery—write 40 words or less that answer the following question: How are you different from your competition?

Now, look critically at every word and phrase you wrote. Draw a line through everything that isn't proven as stated: words like "work hard, dedicated, high quality, lowest cost, save money, proactive" and of course, the more obvious yawners like "best, biggest, fastest, professional," etc.

CHAPTER 5—THE INNER CIRCLE

Now, to the next circle of confusion: features, advantages, and benefits.

In 28 years of training professional people, we have yet to find one person or one firm that knows the difference between features, advantages, and benefits beyond the theoretical explanation. They do not understand that feature-advantage-benefit means attribute-action-result. Attribute is the Seller's side; result is the Buyer's side.

The stuff you sell is dramatically different from how you sell it. The difference between features, advantages, and benefits goes to the absolute center of communicating from the Buyer's point of view. Understanding the differences among them is the fork in the road. The "features-advantages" road keeps you comfortably in your own country; the "benefits" road crosses the Rubicon to the Buyer's interests where new money is waiting.

Features are the attributes of the service a firm offers. The features of your product or service are its facts, data, information, research, history, magnitude, size, shape, color, longevity, smooth shifting, anti-knock, fireproof, natural blond, Dynel, Harvard-educated, 100-year-old company,

$20-billion corporation, walnut paneling, 5,000 partners, 43 offices, penthouse suite, fuel technology, help desk people, server software, granite-faced building, German engineering, MBA, Ph.D., CPA, etc.

Advantages are how the attributes work, how they are transferred to the Buyer, the methods of conveyance, and the actions created by the attributes. For example: "We help corporations refine and execute their business strategy."

Benefits are the business and personal rewards for the Buyer; how it changes or impacts the Buyer's business and personal life. For example: "We help companies save 3,000 hours of management time annually and increase cash flow by 5%."

Your benefits are how your product or service affects the Buyer's business or personal life— increases security, gives them power to make informed decisions, makes them sexier, increases their income by 16%, saves them 30 minutes a day, builds ego and importance, reduces stress level, improves sales, increases market share, increases comfort, improves life style, increases cash flow, etc.

Features, advantages, and benefits form a nervous ménage a trois—who's doing what to whom?

Which part is for the Seller? Which part is for the Buyer? How does it all work? Who's on first?

Professionals solve the Buyer's problems with their stuff—features and advantages—but persuade with the benefits of their stuff.

There are four benefits: power, profit, prestige, and pleasure. At the executive level, however, the most important benefits (and the most convincing) are about time and money—additional profit, ROI, risks reduced, man-hours saved, productivity improved, etc. These benefits need to be quantified with math—dollars, percentages, and ratios—in order to be believed, to show context, to be remembered by the Buyer, and to make the Seller sound like a pro. You will rarely get lost if you take this road. It is a wide, well-marked highway.

The rules: Features and benefits always go together. You may sell benefits alone. Do not sell features alone. The more benefits you sell, the more likely you are to connect with the Buyer. The more features you sell, the more likely your competitor will connect with the Buyer.

Using an earthy analogy, features discuss "This is how we make a baby!" The Buyer covers his eyes and says, "I don't want to watch the process of making the baby—JUST SHOW ME THE BABY!"

The executive-level Buyer would like to know what quantifiable business benefit is being offered: How is my world going to change if I hire these people?

Look back and find the business benefits in our previous examples. Can't find them? You're right.

Even when Duke discusses its features, we can't tell if it sells consulting services, educational services, strategy development services, or whatever. Are these workshops, lectures, seminars, coaching, online distance learning? What? The page is mislabeled. It isn't about benefits for the Client. The correct title is *Features and Advantages for Us*.

So how *might* Duke's message sound for the executive-level Buyer? Something along these lines:

> Duke Corporate Education recruits teams of business experts to help corporations refine and execute their business strategy to save an average of 3000 hours of management time annually and increase cash flow by 3% to 5% based on our past performance with other clients.

We invented this since there is no hint of a Buyer's story on its web site. We suggest this is what interests executive-level Buyers. Using this idea they could have saved pages of copy.

To net it out: from the Buyer's point of view, the businesses in our examples work hard to sell the wrong stuff. Rarely is there ever a mention of the Buyer's side of the equation; it is typical of most firms' disconnection from their Buyers.

Conventional wisdom creates these simple, if feckless, messages, and the other conditions fit; it is convenient because it is second nature for professionals to write (and talk) obscurely; it is comfortable because the competitors in this business write and talk like this; it is comforting because it makes the professionals feel important because this is the language they use to talk to each other; it makes them one of the gang. So these selling messages are all about the Sellers, the self-serving "Glories of Us."

See the problem? When everyone puffs their features and advantages, there is no way to differentiate them, even though they are probably very different in approach, programs, and results. Are these people smart, with brilliant money-making ideas to offer their Buyers? Of course, but you can't tell it by reading their advertising because it is both anti-factual and non-informative.

What most Sellers call "benefits" are actually features or advantages expressed in terms of puffery.

Loving Features

We all love the features of our stuff. Features have been our whole life—inventing them, financing them, improving them, massaging them, caressing and admiring them, meeting about them, market-testing them, and trying to get other people excited about them. From the Buyer's point of view, the features you have so carefully developed aren't the most important part of what you sell. Studying features makes up 94% of corporate training. Because you know too much about your stuff, it's easy to become confused and get in your own way.

Management loves features because benefits are a foreign language to them and the benefit vocabulary is rarely used. MBAs love features. Engineers love features. Consultants love features. Lawyers love features. Indeed, a large part of America's work force is involved with turning out new features. We have seen businesses go bust because they wouldn't discuss any subject but features. So they presented their features to what they belatedly discovered was a completely uninterested market.

Trade shows are delightful venues to watch companies work hard to look and sound like their competitors. Shows are filled with acronyms, model numbers, new and improved widgets. All features.

It is easy to center a firm's efforts entirely on the technical side of the business. Technical skills and innovation are the ante in the competitive game. They are not the game itself—the game is persuasion—protecting or gaining market share.

Then there is the invention-development-improvement-improvement-improvement circle, which is management-inspired and engineer-driven.

Modern life is one continuous upgrade path. Your Buyer expects it. Your salespeople expect it. Your competitors expect it. We see managers mesmerized (and paralyzed) by the constant race to create new features for their stuff. Surprisingly, there seems to be little long-term selling advantage created by all these new features since the competitors usually match them within months, often within weeks, or in the case of software, days.

Hot new features presented without benefits offer only an unreliable short-term advantage. Translating new features ("our new software") into the impact on the Buyer's business ("reduces costs of your operations by 4%") gives context to the feature. Do not confuse your new features with a persuasive, benefits-filled story. Developing hot new features without a translation into Buyer-benefit language is an exciting way to waste a bunch of money.

When playing the persuasion game, obviously one uses benefits far more than features.

Hidden Money

In business, there are both above-the-line and below-the-line benefits.

Above-the-line benefits include obvious things like:

- Increase profits by 18%

- Reduce costs by $200,000

- Save 10 hours a month or 120 hours a year

- Reduce labor by 21%

- Outperform the market 4 to 1

- Companies that run SAP are 32% more profitable.[9]

Below-the-line benefits are less obvious and address losses, both existing and potential. They mitigate or prevent liabilities through the use of your services. Things like:

- Reduce capital investments by as much 30%

- Prevent operating losses that could be as much as $2 million

- Prevent two weeks of downtime a year

- Reduce potential liabilities costing as much as $400,000

- Reduce risk by 350%

- Avoid noncompliance fines of as much as $50 million

Don't overlook below-the-line benefits. They offer great opportunities to differentiate your services from the rest. Sellers as a group love "happy talk," so below-the-line benefits are rarely discussed or even recognized by them. (Notice that insurance companies own most of the big buildings. They sell mostly below the line—defending against things that might happen.)

If you have a firm that is famous in its field, that fame—brand equity—is the additional perceived value the Buyer places on your firm; it is the promise of a predictable level of performance.

Virtually all of a firm's brand equity is rooted in below-the-line benefits. They allow Buyers to feel secure doing business with you—it reduces their perceived risk, and is the reason many people choose one firm over another. (Nobody ever got fired for buying IBM.)

For CEOs, CFOs, and others in the executive suites of our nation, the biggest thrill of the past few years was seeing fellow corporate executives doing the "perp walk." The impact of those television images of handcuffed men in bespoke suits shuffling along to jail in the company of giant cops was—how should we say this—sobering. Keeping executives in compliance and out of the hands of gun-toting government employees is a very compelling below-the-line benefit.

Features and benefits are binary: on or off, black or white, yes or no, you or me, Seller or Buyer— no middle ground because from the Buyer's point of view, there is no middle ground. You are either on the Buyer's side (benefits) or you are not (features).

Reality Check: The Important Benefit

Ask your salespeople, "What important benefits do you sell to your Buyer?" The answer will be a list of features. Occasionally you will run into some hot dog who will slip in an advantage or two. But you will hear no benefits.

When you point out that they listed features not benefits, they sometimes correct themselves and begin to add what they think are benefits to the list. Except they will not be benefits but additional features or advantages. Professionals will talk features until your eyes glaze over. Unfortunately, that is the torture they inflict on their Buyers, also.

● ●

I bought the first Macintosh computer I laid eyes on; bought it on the spot in 1986. I didn't buy it because I was a computer weenie. I hate computers. I bought it because I was in business and it would make my work easier.

On that premise, Apple's advertising, selling proposition, and benefits package might have been something along the lines of:

Easy to use, intuitive—talk with your own brain instead of with the computer

Highly productive—novice can produce a work product in under 30 minutes

Fast learning curve—2 hours of training per program vs. 8 hours for competition

Not frustrating—can't easily lose work due to operator error, etc.

Instead, they sold engineering, the bells and whistles, of this marvelous little life-changer. They fought their way up to an 8% market share against other features-driven PC manufacturers. And they kept improving the features and selling the features not benefits. The result is that Apple will go down as one of the great missed business opportunities of the last century because they tried to sell the features of their revolutionary idea rather than the dramatic benefits which they monopolized: pain-free ease of use with high productivity. (The graphic user interface features were not copied until ten years later by Microsoft Windows.)

Apple had the correct engineering concept: build a computer that doesn't require one's thumb to be permanently stuck into a book of documentation. They started with human terms: "A computer for the rest of us!" But then they lost their way when the engineers and marketers took over. They commoditized their genius, selling Ram and Rom and interface and SCSI and chip speed. Just like all their PC competitors.

Apple failed to capitalize on their ten-year monopoly because they thought they were in the computer hardware business. They could have asked any Mac user and learned that from the Buyer's point of view Apple was in the "increase production" and "feel-good-about-work" business; the "don't-be-frustrated" and "don't-do-work-over-again-because-you-lost-it" business; the "who-the-hell-wants-to-talk-computer-language" and "you-don't-have-to-be-afraid-of-this-computer" business; the "you-don't-need-a-live-in-support-person" business.

From the Buyer's point of view, when Apple started they were alone, unique in the elegance of their idea. Then they chose to be another face in the crowd. They turned "The Computer for the Rest of Us"—their first ad slogan—into "The Computer Just Like the Rest of Them". They lost sight of their guiding star—simple and intuitive usability.

Had Apple approached the market in human terms rather than engineering terms, benefits rather than features, they would have owned a huge market share today. At this writing, Apple's market share is under 3%. They are still selling bells and whistles.

● ●

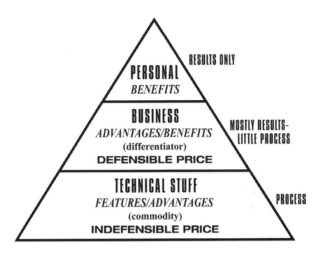

THE THREE LEVELS OF PERSUASION: EACH MORE PERSUASIVE
AND PROFITABLE THE HIGHER YOU GO.

The technical, or **stuff** level, is the lowest
common denominator of persuasion. It inhabits
the heavily populated real estate at the bottom of
the selling pyramid where everyone brags about
themselves. At this low level, stuff is explained by
features with an advantage or two—process—how
it works.

Because most sellers inhabit this low-rent section
of town, stuff becomes a commodity. As a
commodity, it is nearly impossible to get more

than the market fee (the "competitive" price) for anything. Everybody's got stuff. Nobody's impressed.

The **business** level is a much less crowded neighborhood since few firms actually visit there. Business is discussed as a few advantages but mostly results in the form of the benefits like time and money. Because this neighborhood has little traffic, your firm can stand out, that is, become a differentiator. As a differentiator your fee is defensible—you can ask and receive a higher fee— the "value" price.

The **personal** level is rarified air. Few firms or their salespeople ever get to breathe it. (While they insist that they do, salespeople actually know little about the Buyer's personal life, which makes the idea of relationship a hollow one.) Behind every business decision lurks a personal agenda. This is a pure benefit sale, how the Buyer is personally impacted by the results created by your stuff.

Chapter 7—Business Myths

"Myth: an ill-founded belief held uncritically especially by an interested group. Mythical: fabricated, invented, or imagined in an arbitrary way in defiance of facts."

—Merriam-Webster Dictionary

Ultimately, business success lies in dealing with reality rather than fantasy.

Over time, myths become conventional wisdom because no one refutes them. While training more than 12,000 highly educated professional and executive salespeople inside the crucible of a demanding, difficult, and sometimes contentious classroom, and for ten years closely tracking the actions of a third of them, the high price of believing in selling illusions becomes stunningly obvious.[10]

Our observations seem outrageous since many of them directly challenge conventional wisdom. Many myths, while couched in business terms, are really preciously held beliefs to be mightily defended by your salespeople and marketers. So don't take our word for anything in this book; test everything for yourself.

Here are some expensive myths that are widely accepted as established truth.

MYTH 1

Sell yourself first

This myth is seen as an undisputable truth, yet in 12,000 tries, we have never found anyone who could convincingly sell themselves first. Like levitation, it's impossible, but it's a ton of fun to watch people try to fly.

Professionals are often surprised to learn that Buyers don't care about them, their lives, their recent divorce, their dog, their kids, their boat, or their Telluride hot-tub vacation. The *only* thing the Buyer cares about is what's in the transaction for him.

Executives have little time to invest in the Seller's small talk, which makes the underlying premise of selling yourself first exactly wrong. Even great execution cannot save a poor idea.

If you don't sell yourself first, then what do you open with? Buyer benefits, of course.

Myth 2

Our Buyers come first

This evergreen philosophy is supposed to signal executive Buyers that your company is compulsively attentive to them. This philosophy is seriously undermined by the arrogance many firms and their professionals unconsciously project.

Seventy percent of professionals become fidgety and uncomfortable when listening to the executive Buyer explain what their problems are and what and how they would like to be sold.

From the professionals we often hear, "They (the Buyers) talk about subjects I'm not interested in and I get bored. I pretend to listen but I'd rather not." They do not look at the Buyer's side of the transaction or how their services alter the Buyer's world. Many consultants are arrogant, condescending, and unwilling to make the Buyer feel good about doing business with them.

They don't let the Buyer talk; they rarely inquire about the Buyer's real business or personal problems; they relentlessly opine; they bore their Buyers to death. Actually, for most firms, customers come second. The "glories of us" come first.

Myth 3

The Buyer is always right

This is so obviously untrue as to be laughable. Buyers are often wrong about everything from the weather to the economy.

They have old information, misinformation, partial facts, misperceptions, and misunderstandings. But they are always right about their business and personal issues, their vision, feelings, ambitions, and they always have the money… and you don't.

Buyers should be treated with kid gloves and respect while their misperceptions are gently excised.

Myth 4

We want to partner with our Clients

In business, the word partnership means to share financial responsibilities, that is, both profits and losses generated. Your offer to become partners prompts the Buyer's question, "Mr. Seller, what portion of my liabilities will you assume to get my business?" We have never met a Seller who wanted to be a partner after carefully thinking out this rather silly offer.

When these exchanges are decoded, they read: The Buyer is looking for a good, attentive, trustworthy, professional service provider who under-promises and over-delivers. The last thing the Buyer is looking for is another partner. Partners are a pain in the ass. He has plenty of partners he must answer to without you.

Myth 5

We have great relationships with our Clients

Conventional wisdom holds that building a relationship with the Buyer is a prerequisite to a sale. This is untrue; this is a trap and the nuances are endless.

Trying to build a relationship before the sale puts the cart before the horse. Performance comes first; the relationship second. Personal connections are built on actual performance, not promises, not expensive dinners, not basketball tickets, or remembered birthdays.

Building a relationship with a new Buyer takes time because trust—the basis of friendship—must be established first. The Buyer's trust is created and maintained by the fulfillment of promises made by the Seller, the firm, and the marketing. Trustworthy relationships are created after you have proven you are worthy of trust.

Once you are a proven performer, however, you may make friends for life. Some of my best friends are current and former clients. In the beginning, we made promises to them. Then we spared no effort to keep those promises. Over time, they trusted what we said and our business acquaintanceship grew into personal friendship.

Now, we like them for who they are; we would still like them if they never gave us another dime of business. Our jokes would be just as bad, our laughs just as deep, and our affection just as genuine.

Buyers tell us they have little or no interest in building a relationship with a service provider. (And many times, vice versa.) The executive-level Buyers we talk with aren't looking for faux friends. What Buyers want is someone to help them solve their business problems and their personal problems caused by business. On a level playing field, the Buyer will buy from a person he knows or likes or is a person like them; the Seller's job is to un-level the playing field with a compelling story. Buyers will buy from a gorilla in a pink tutu if the tritzy gorilla will solve their problems.

When friendship is a commodity bought and sold, the highest bidder wins—whoever gives away the best sports tickets, shares the most fees, parties on the fanciest boat, or is a member of the best golf club—owns the buyer's business until a higher bidder comes along.

The problem with overly close relationships for the Seller is that business eventually suffers. When you are having too much fun on the golf course there is a natural reticence to close new business. That reticence allows the competitors to walk in and solve the Buyer's real problem that you overlooked while smoking, joking, and playing pinochle at the nineteenth hole.

From the Buyer's point of view, a consultant's attempt to "build a personal relationship" complicates the Buyer's decision making, adding unnecessary stress for the Buyer because Buyers want to reserve the right to fire you; it is hard to fire your friends with a clear conscience. Often, friends are squeezed out of business because a stranger comes along with a better story and more Buyer consciousness. And better sports tickets.

In groups of professionals, we asked for a show of hands from those that thought they had a close Buyer relationship and still lost business to outsiders: 100%.

Pursuing business at the relationship level is tough because both Buyer and Seller know that this faux friendship is about money. A close friendship actually lowers your fee. The Client says, "Because we have this long-term relationship, we think you ought to give us a break."

The professional who relies on a relationship for ongoing business needs to schedule lots of prayer time. There is a name for people who sell their friendship. This isn't lost on the Buyer, and the Seller is judged accordingly.

●●●●●●●●●●●●●●●●●●●●●●●●●●●●●●●●●●

This story from a frustrated senior partner of a consulting firm:

"One of our clients called and said he had a problem that must be handled in a matter of hours—a problem which would normally take us days. Putting our regular work on hold, we assigned everyone in the office to the crash project. With superhuman effort, we made their impossible deadline. They were very happy. We then said, "Because we have such a great relationship with you, we are going to reduce our fee by 25%.

"We delivered service above and beyond the call of duty and then cut our fee voluntarily. They never even asked what the fee would be. Makes no sense whatsoever."

●●●●●●●●●●●●●●●●●●●●●●●●●●●●●●●●●●

MYTH 6

We are the best in the business

Actually, everyone in a category of business is
perceived as average (or the best depending on
how you look at it), not only in the Buyer's eyes
but in his own. When we ask different firms in the
same industry, "Compared to your competitors,
how would you rank the quality of your firm and
its services: in the top third, middle, or lower
third?" Everyone's answer is always the same:
"Top third," which, of course, in reality makes
them all equal, and interchangeable—congruent
with the Buyer's perception which is "Everyone is
pretty good."

Highest quality is a concept that managers like
and marketing people love. Conventional wisdom
says that the Buyer carefully chooses and buys
from the most qualified firm. Actually, the Buyer
usually can't tell one firm from another because
they all sound alike. The idea of being "the best"
is spurious: only a tiny percentage of Buyers care—
the connoisseurs and collectors. And how can they
tell if what you sell is really the best? What is the
practical test? Settling for "good enough" is part
of the human wiring. It allows Buyers to make

efficient decisions based on whatever works to solve their immediate problem.

Myth 7

We know our business

Seventy-six percent of salespeople are unable to define their Clients' larger business problems that are solved by the Seller's products and services.

Professionals are experts in their field and their overabundance of technical knowledge often gets in the way of getting hired; their presentation about their expertise is inadvertently designed to obfuscate, not clarify; complicate, not simplify. Eighty-nine percent do not understand what business they are really in from their Client's point of view.

For most professionals, recognizing the following law leaves a scuff mark on the brain.

LAW OF PROFESSIONAL CREDENTIALS

Credentials are worthless in the marketplace if you can't explain how they create money for the Buyer.

Myth 8

Our business is different
Our business is the same

"Our business is different" is usually the manager's position about his firm; it has different processes or approaches that (it is hoped) differentiate the firm and its offerings. This message is loudly and relentlessly proclaimed in sales meetings and boardrooms.

"Our business is the same" describes the feeling (or certain knowledge) of the people who sell the stuff. Usually, these subversive admissions come to us in private, whispered conversations well out of management's hearing. Many salespeople believe that, in spite of hoping to appear different in the Buyer's eyes, it is ultimately impossible because their stuff is the same as the competitors'.

They are both right because both points of view center on features, not benefits.

In our experience, many times there are dramatic differences among businesses in the same industry even if they can't explain those differences to their Buyers. Nearly every business is unique in some way or at least different enough from the pack that with some decoding and translation into a Buyer's story, each can be perceived not as a commodity but as a firm different from all the rest.

Just *saying* your firm is different doesn't make it different. From the outside, where the Buyer lives, unless there is a differentiating story, all businesses are the same. Perception is reality. The Buyer's *perception* of a company is the controlling factor. Perceptions can be changed with a story for the Buyer.

So the paradox is that while all businesses, like people, are pretty much the same in the DNA, at the level above that there are many benefits that can differentiate the way in which companies are perceived by the market.

MYTH 9

We are great salespeople

Most people who think of themselves as salespeople are actually order takers. In fact, 92% of buying decisions are made before the Buyer condescends to discuss things with a vendor. This fact would imply the Seller would ask questions and listen to the answers. Instead, professionals spend most of their time talking and wrecking, not making, sales.

Ninety-six percent of professionals never challenge the aphorisms and popular illusions about selling, no matter how illogical, mythical, or wishful, especially those generated within the closed circle of their own profession.

Sometimes there is confusion between selling talent and economic conditions. When the economy is booming, marginal businesses can survive, look successful, and even prosper. When the world is awash in money, Buyers are more carefree and uncritical about their decisions. Bankers and venture capitalists go all funny in the head and throw capital at inept managers and half-baked concepts, rolling the dice.

In a hyperactive world, people lose their perspective; the economic flood tide covers up poor skills and grievous mistakes. Management takes credit for being great managers when, in fact, their boat is rising with everyone else's and has little to do with their business acumen. They are passengers in the boat but believe they are steering.

As Warren Buffet says, "When the tide goes out, you can see who has been swimming naked."

In 2000, the tide went out and everyone saw that the dot-coms had been skinny-dipping along with the telecom industry and energy traders and overpaid executives and stockholders and analysts and fund managers; they had been bobbing around nakedly on the high tide high-fiving each other's brilliance.

A world awash in cash covers sins and distorts perspective. Many of the large bankruptcies we see are the result of perfect world businesses. WorldCom, Enron and Global Crossing were run by crooks whose tracks were easily covered by the mysteries of technology. Conseco, United Airlines, and others had incompetence covered by the same inundation of green. There will be more. There is a difference between naughtiness and stupidity but the results are the same.

A business that can survive only in a perfect world with perfect playing conditions faces doom as the business environment inevitably turns imperfect. When their market fails, managers can't get their foot off the cost accelerator fast enough to keep from hitting the wall. Believing that the perfect world is the way life is, they never develop a Plan B. They crash at high speed.

Myth 10

We use the consultative selling style

The concept of "consultative selling" is a no-brainer. Like skydiving, skiing, or windsurfing, everyone has the concept but we find that fewer than 11% of professional salespeople can actually persuade in a consultative manner. Salespeople confuse the desire to be consultative with having the mechanical skills to actually do it.

● ●

My longtime architect friend was on the building committee of a $50-million museum complex. The committee interviewed seven general contractors and narrowed the field to two, both well-qualified. But my architect friend preferred one by a thin margin and carefully instructed his choice contractor to say these words in the final committee meeting: "What would you like your contractor to do that would keep you, the client-owner, happy with this project?"

After the presentation, the architect said, "Why didn't you say what I suggested you say? If you had, you would have won."

The contractor said, "But...I did."

The architect replied, "No, you didn't. You may think you did, but you didn't. You and your team talked about yourselves and your credentials the whole time. That's why you lost. You had this deal in the bag if you had just asked them what they expected from their general contractor and listened to the opinions of the committee."

● ●

Professionals honestly believe they ask these kinds of global questions. They almost never do because they are secretly afraid of what the Buyer might say. Professionals believe that if Buyers never actually say aloud what they think, then they must not think it. Just because it remains unspoken doesn't mean it remains unthought. Just because it is thought doesn't mean it is spoken.

The reason consultative selling is difficult is that salespeople (especially highly educated professionals) pitch. They have never been taught the mechanics of asking intelligent questions and listening to the answers, the baseline moves of good conversation.

Getting inside the Buyer's mind is rather simple if you put aside the concept of "pitching." When a salesperson learns not to pitch, indeed, doesn't call it pitching even when talking with peers, consultative selling becomes easier to learn and do because it is simply civilized conversation between two people working on a problem one of them has.

The single trait that makes a great salesperson is curiosity. Many professionals are curiously incurious about their Buyer. Decoded, consultative selling means "no pitching." It also means being insatiably curious.

Myth 11

We create win-win solutions

This is less of a myth and more of a fraud.

While this is a feel-good concept, we have never seen a firm that can explain what winning means from the Buyer's side, if the firm actually solved the Buyer's business problem, or how to express the value of the firm's solution in business terms. So how does a firm really know if the Buyer wins or not?

Many Sellers have researched the Buyer's attitudes about their own products and services but have never researched the Buyer's results. In customer surveys the Sellers ask, in one form or another, "How did we do?"—an all-about-us question. The real question (perhaps the only important one) is "How did you do using our services?" The research upon which to build a Buyer's story is derived from the all-about-them question. "How did your business change in dollars, ratios, or percentages of additional revenues, savings, profits, etc.?"

Because Sellers have no reality-based sense of their performance record or how their services fit into the Buyer's business, they can't discuss performance in quantifiable terms. Further, they have little idea of how the firm's history of results impacts the Buyer's decision making. Then, when a Seller flashes a client-list and the prospect asks, "What happened for them?" the Sellers have no definitive, provable, quantified answer. Who knows who wins?

Myth 12

We are skillful negotiators

Ninety-three percent of professionals will volunteer to cut their fee without being asked. Eighty-four percent believe their products and services are too expensive, anyway.

Consultants and businesspeople have taken their reduction to a commodity as a fact of life. In private conversations, even highly paid consultants confess that in their heart-of-hearts, they believe everyone in their business is the same and probably overpaid at that.

According to the our study, 97% of Sellers will take what they are "awarded" without a hint of resistance and be delighted that the Buyer blesses them with business.

Unless one has quantified benefits there is nothing to trade the Buyer. It is impossible to negotiate without trading stock (discussed later).

Myth 13

Bring a deal anywhere near us and we'll make it happen

Seventy-seven percent of professionals won't close a transaction when the Buyer is ready to hire them. Professionals can't take yes for an answer; it is hard to buy from them.

Professionals tell us the reason they call at the executive level is to "tell them about us" or "introduce ourselves" or "put a face to the name."

What professionals often do not comprehend is that executives make deals and hire outside vendors all day every day. That is what they do for a living. The Seller is just part of the daily parade of potential deals an executive accepts or rejects.

So they talk past each other. Many professionals have been offered engagements only to walk away because they insisted on vomiting their whole boring story, could not hear what the Buyer was saying, and forgot that they were in the room to get hired.

In every meeting, somebody gets sold. Sometimes it's them; sometimes it's you.

Myth 14

We are always looking for an edge

Forty-eight percent of professionals are satisfied with their current level of performance and income, and they accept high loss ratios as a fact of life. And after all, they are looking only for their fair share.

Everybody likes to win. Few prepare to win the selling game.

Eighty-two percent of Sellers are willing to accept a ninety percent rejection rate.

Myth 15

Become an expert and the world is your oyster

The world is overpopulated with experts. Today, expertise is expected. Credentials are a given. Degrees are normal.

For the professional to do what she loves, her expertise, no matter how finely tuned, must first be sold either by the professional person herself or by someone else. Selling comes first, expertise second.

Actually, most professionals would prefer that someone else do it. Many chose their profession precisely because they erroneously believed they would never have to lower themselves to sell. Alas, in today's environment, bringing in new business is a prerequisite to moving up in a professional firm. For the professionals, the higher you climb the tougher the competition and the more selling skills required to fend off competitors and mine current clients (both inside and outside the firm.) Result: no selling, no partnership distributions, no oyster.

Compensation plans are the elephant in the room because they often discourage a person's individual selling effort. The firm's compensation plan signals what the managers believe is important to the firm. If management respects technical expertise more than people skills, then individual selling initiative and the resulting new clients are harder to come by.

To encourage new business development, management has first to publicly admit that personal selling skills are as important as technical expertise and reward accordingly.

Myth 16

Build a better mousetrap and the world will beat a path to your door

Sounds good but it ain't true. Companies go broke believing that a good product sells itself. Ralph Waldo Emerson's mousetrap line shows that while he was a pretty good writer, when it came to business, he was an out-of-touch, ivory-tower, fuzzy-thinking geek who never spent time selling on the street.

We have the most sophisticated buying and selling economy in history. And when Ralph wrote his ode to inventiveness, having a superior product was quite enough, thank you. This is a different world. The idea of commanding a market because you have a superior product or service is an artifact of a gentler, more romantic time.

Life is one continuous upgrade path. Today, most mousetraps are excellent; as Buyers, we expect state-of-the-art design, the newest feature, the latest upgrade, the hottest service, an exact fit, the most personal attention. We expect superior products and services from every company in the marketplace.

Management must be able to explain the benefits of its new and improved mousetrap in words that the Buyer can understand. If it cannot, management ends up with a warehouse full of beautifully designed, but unsold death machines in blister packs labeled "Spring Time for Mr. Mouse."

CHAPTER 8—MARCHING TO THE HUMDRUM

Within the top-tier firms in your industry or profession:

- Everyone is an expert.

- Everyone has a great track record.

- Everyone sounds alike and works hard to do so.

- No one can defend his asking price.

- Every company is unique and can't explain why.

- No salesperson believes these facts apply to him.

This commonality makes salespeople in every industry or profession sound exactly like their competitors, a commodity by anyone's definition.

This "me-tooism" can cost a company one-quarter to one-half of its sales revenues. It makes firms with outstanding people and superior knowledge interchangeable with the worst of its competitors and accepting the lowest fee. Those lost dollars are baked into the cultural cake by B-schools, advertising and marketing types, salespeople fighting to survive, and the technical people who honestly believe that Buyers really care about the same stuff they care about. (This information and its Reality Checks should be built-in to every B-School business case. Our experience shows that business school graduates are frightfully lacking in these skills.)

Sellers habitually sell at too low a level, down at the level of influencers where both the Seller and Buyer are comfortable with conversations about stuff rather than persuading at the executive level where the big dollar decisions are ultimately made. At the executive level, unless decoded, "stuff pitches" are a waste of time.

Giving Up the High Ground

Professionals get hired because of their asymmetrical information, i.e., the difference between the seller's expertise about a given subject and the Buyer's expertise about the same subject. The higher the asymmetry, the higher the fee a professional can charge.

Professionals seem driven by some dark force to reduce the asymmetry. The more detail professionals divulge about the processes they use, the narrower the gap. Conventional wisdom calls this "educating the Buyer." By closing the gap, they reduce their fee; they voluntarily come down from the tree-covered high ground and stand on the barren flats with their run-of-the-mill competitors.

The Buyer assumes that professional asymmetry exists and wants it to remain so. What the Buyer wants to know is what the professional's expertise will do for the Buyer. What is it going to cost? What will the Buyer get for his money?

We use a Dr. Business analogy: A ballet dancer goes to her doctor and says, "Doctor, my leg hurts."

The doctor says, "Here is what we are going to do.

"We'll bring you in Friday morning, shave your leg with a low-friction, epidermal, hypoallergenic razor. We'll then give you 10cc of Nervocaine— delivered with an autoclavable, latex-free syringe and a metal-hubbed needle with PSX-coated technology.

"Then we'll take a gamma-radiated, size 12, carbon steel scalpel, just like this one, slice through the epidermis and dermis until we get to the tibia.

"Using a Zimmer orthopaedic bone saw with foot switch—the number one bone saw in the world—we'll then grind through the tibia until we reach the bone marrow where we will extract 10cc of bone marrow gel with a size 8 piston syringe before stitching you up with a drilled-end, counter-sunk, corrosion-resistant needle and 2.5 feet of Chromic catgut sutures and send you back upstairs to await the results."

The patient holds her head in her hands and thinks, "Ugh. This is a lot more than I wanted to know. Maybe my leg doesn't hurt that much."

Professional service firms delight in sharing every detail of the pending operation with their Buyers. Information dumps are consultants' favorite pastime; opining is their stock in trade. Virtually every professional services firm we have encountered sells like this, methodically reducing the asymmetry while the patient holds her head in her hands and wonders if it's worth the pain.

CHAPTER 9—TRANSLATION

If one ignores conventional wisdom, it is fairly easy to discern that the Buyer's interest and agenda—and the Seller's interest and agenda—often compete; the points of view often differ; their interests conflict.

Many times the Buyer is the competition: "We'll do this ourselves." Each time the Buyer decides to buy, he must make a choice between your offerings, the competitors' offerings, doing it himself, or not doing it at all.

The story professionals love to tell day and night (and unfortunately do) is their story from their own point of view. Of course, this story makes all professionals in their industry sound exactly alike; it converts talented, creative, unique, and highly educated people into interchangeable suppliers.

So the first problem that must be solved is to figure out what you, your services, and your firm do for the Buyer. Building a business story from the Buyer's point of view is a completely different story than the business story you tell now.

So let's approach the positioning problem with the Buyer in mind.

SELLER'S vs. POINT OF VIEW	vs.	BUYER'S POINT OF VIEW
My stuff	vs.	Ego, money, power, security, sex appeal, etc.
Corporate	vs.	Personal
Information	vs.	Reasons to buy
Inside focus/ me	vs.	Me/inside focus
My agenda	vs.	My agenda
Process	vs.	Results

We have discovered that most organizations, both big and small, either present a poor face to the market or none at all. Their standard, and wholly predictable, position is "We do everything for everybody at any time at the lowest price."

This comes forth in comfortable phrases like, "general brokerage," "full service," and "highest quality." This happens even in the face of common knowledge that a specialist gets paid more than the generalist and that in the Buyer's mind, doing everything for everybody really means "Everything we do is average." All-inclusive language in a company's position signals to the Buyer, "We'll try anything if you pay for it."

The Buyer's perception of your firm, its services, and your fee are inextricably linked and the natural result of being perceived as average: your price suffers.

The Buyer is looking for someone to trust and someone who can do the work at a fair price. (You'll notice we didn't say the lowest price.)

"Positioning" is a catchword made famous by the marketing gurus Ries and Trout. It is the face you show to the marketplace and, like tennis, it relies on hitting the ball where your competition is not.

Trust can be built into your positioning if you sell the benefits of your solution to the Buyer's business problems and everything you say is provable. Thus, understanding the difference between puffery and representation on one hand and features and benefits on the other becomes the Rosetta Stone for breaking the code to the Buyer's mind and allowing trust to conquer the Buyer's culturally acquired cynicism.

With different positioning, you can change the Buyer's perception of your service and the organization behind it; a differentiating position can build trust in your firm and its people and can create an average of 12% more revenue than the competition for comparable products or services.[11]

This "story for the Buyer" is management's opportunity to move outside the closed thinking of the incestuous company culture and into the broad horizons of the Buyer.

The Translations

A number of translations can be used to convert the Seller's story into the Buyer' story:

- Features translate to advantages and benefits.

- Stuff translates to business or personal context.

- Process translates to results.

- Puffery (lies) translates to representation (truth).

- Client-list translates to condensed history.

- Market price translates to asking price.

- Relationship translates to quantified benefits.

With these translations, your firm can transform itself from a commodity into a differentiator which brings the question, "Can't all our competitors do this?" The answer is yes, they can, but it is a rare firm that expends energy on this subject. They make a couple of passes at the problem, get bored, and go to lunch.

By visiting their web sites, it is easy to deduce how managers and marketers think. Few firms say how they impact the Buyer's business in any quantifiable way. It is not revealed.

You doubt this? Tour their web sites.

Visit Lucent Technology (www.lucent.com). Its story is "Deliver more value over IP™." Then the full explanation: "Lucent's Convergence Solutions enable the blended lifestyle services subscribers demand...."

Now there is an irresistible proposition that makes one tremble in anticipation.

Is there a connection between this lack of cogent story and Lucent's stock price?

For a year, we polled our students—mostly lawyers, consultants, MBAs, and CPAs—in our executive-level workshops: "What does Lucent do for a living?" That question produces blank stares. Then one person out of twenty will answer, "Telecom."

"What's telecom?" we ask. There are no answers to this deeply complex question.

Here's my conclusion: Because Lucent did not translate its story into Buyer benefits, it wasted millions on advertising and the stock tanked. (The price was north of $60 in 1999 and south of three bucks in 2005.) One of the most prestigious businesses in the country—this was Bell Laboratories, for goodness' sake—a shining example of the best inventive environment America has to offer. It owns thousands of patents and files more every day.

When a company markets its stuff, it is asking Buyers to invest their time and attention. If the message is not stated in terms Buyers understand, they don't invest their mental energy and eventually they ignore these mystery companies.

Products and services alone do not make a stock valuable—it is the Buyer's perception that makes stock valuable, a story that separates it from the background clutter of the competition and gives the Buyer a sense of how the stuff fits into the Buyer's life. Without a Buyer's context, a marketing message is just more white noise to be filtered out.

Warren Buffett, the master investor, says, "I don't invest in businesses I don't understand."

Ol' Warren doesn't own Lucent stock. Perhaps it's because he can't understand what the firm does. It makes one wonder if Lucent knows itself. Its web site indicates that Lucent may not.

Just tour around the Internet and at each home page ask the following questions:

- What do these people do for a living?

- What's in this for me as a potential Buyer?

- How does this impact my life? How will my life be different if I hire these people or use their stuff?

- Do I get a sense of magnitude from its promise or find a quantified business benefit?

- Can I understand the message in four seconds or less? (A full-page ad in *The New York Times* gets four seconds of attention.)

Visit BASF. (www.basf.com) "BASF is the world's leading chemical company. We aim to increase and sustain our corporate value through growth and innovation."

So what's in that for the Buyer? This web site is written for BASF's navel gazing.

If you had visited AT&T's site before it was absorbed by a smaller firm, you would have seen nothing but the words: "Consumer. Business. Wireless. Broadband." That's it. Not even a weak attempt to project a message for the Buyer.

In the conference room, AT&T looked into its own innards and divined a profound truth that everybody knew about the company and what it did for a living. How could any thinking American think otherwise?

Obviously AT&T didn't speak to its Buyers. It continued to lose ground. In 2005, the moribund company disappeared, absorbed by SBC Communications, which renamed itself AT&T.

Now you can visit AT&T's new, improved web site at http://www.att.com: "AT&T's passion to invent and SBC's drive to deliver have come together to create the most complete and secure network delivering what matters most in your world. Introducing the new AT&T."

A symphony of noninformation; an ode to vagueness.

Visit Citigroup. "This is Citigroup. 102 countries, 120 currencies." OK, so you are big and international. What's in it for me? What do you do? Those questions remain unanswered on the home page.

Here are some firms that know what they do:

Google delivers accurate information in eight-tenths of a second. I can understand that.

Amazon.com sells books at a discount and runs 24/7. I've got that.

BP sells gas damned near everywhere. I
understand.

Southern Company sells electricity. Yep.

Drinking Coca-Cola makes me feel like 20 again.

Reality Check

If you can't answer the Buyer's simplest questions
about how your stuff affects his life, then you
don't know what business you are in.

What does your company sell that I as a Buyer can
understand in 20 words or less?

How does what you say impact my life in some
quantifiable way?

Differentiation

"It's not fun to fight conventional wisdom. It makes people angry."

—Steven Levitt, Author, *Freakonomics*

Here are some areas in which a firm can differentiate itself, assuming, of course, that each of these features or advantages is approached from the Buyer's side:

- Market image; position against competition

- Experience; the history and quantified Benefits delivered

- Specialized knowledge

- Focus; Categories of business a firm dominates

- Mission; the internal drive or focus of management

- Staff; quality of employees and support people

- Management philosophy and/or style

- Compensation plans

- Resources; the knowledge, hard assets and infrastructure

- Selection and/or quality of services

- What you sell; quantifiable potential gains, avoided losses

- Risk management,

- Reduction of aggravation dollars (explained later).

Price itself can be an effective market differentiator. The surest way to remain a commodity is to charge the same price as the competition.

When companies don't quantify the benefits of what they sell, we have found that they consistently undercharge by as much as 50% to 200% based on the provable value they deliver to their Buyers. (This observation holds across companies within an industry and across industries.) Without a story of quantifiable results for the Buyer, Sellers stand naked in the price negotiation.

Pooling technical expertise, business experience, market knowledge, business strategy, and quantified Benefits, an organization can design a simple, forcefully positioned, and differentiating competitive selling message. Our clients have found that a well-researched and truthful story is infinitely more powerful than any BS the marketing and salespeople have the nerve to invent.

Universal Business Problems

Every firm faces the same seven business problems, whether it is General Motors, Detroit, Michigan, or Locos Tacos, Ajo, Arizona. How to:

- Acquire and manage **capital**
- Acquire and manage **people**
- Find and fill **markets**
- Meet and exceed the **competition**
- Improve quality and lower costs of **production**
- Maintain sufficient and predictable **cash flow**
- Maintain controlled and predictable **overhead**

When preparing your position, you will be way ahead of the game if your products and services address one or more of these universal business problems.

The Easiest Sale—The Reptilian Mind

There is usually a hard way and easy way to do everything. It is surprising how often businesspeople choose the hard way, especially in sales and marketing.

Executives, like the rest of us, make decisions emotionally. They call it "gut feeling"—and justify their decisions intellectually.

Down deep in their reptilian minds—that most primitive part of the brain which wrestles with problems of food, fighting, fleeing and making babies—CEOs, chief financial officers, and entrepreneurs have additional primal concerns usually spared the rest of us: all day, every day, they are dreadfully anxious about the answers to three essential questions:

- Survival—Will I and my business survive?

- Profit—If I survive, will I make a profit?

- Cash flow—If I survive and make a profit, will I have enough cash flow to pay bills?

The easiest way to sell the upper echelons of business is to help them stop worrying—or at least worry less—about the three questions they sweat over every minute of every day. (We have vetted this idea with a number of CEOs and chief operations officers without a single objection raised. On the contrary, most nod in agreement.)

How do you sell into these worries? By showing executives how to cut costs, increase sales, and improve cash flow—by helping them convert their goods and services to cash more quickly. When you construct your provable benefits to address one or more of these issues, the executive Buyer's attention is riveted on you.

When you help a company become more competitive; gain market share; increase inventory turns; save time or space; reduce employee costs, wages, or insurance premiums; manage risk; reduce absenteeism; increase morale and productivity; or solve related problems, you can sell at the highest levels of business. Our Clients find that this kind of selling, while it takes research and homework, is simple once you understand how.

Because Sellers have little sense of their company's performance record or how it fits into the Buyer's business, they do not know how they impact the Buyer's business or their decision making in the context of survival, profit, and cash flow: the passionate interest of the executive suite.

People further down in the business hierarchy may not have these same do-or-die concerns. Middle managers often have other, more personal agendas, like moving up in the organization, looking good, covering their tail, or getting a raise. They are dreadfully anxious about the answers to the following three essential and ever-present questions:

- Will I survive?
- Will I survive?
- Will I survive?

Obviously, helping these people keep what they have would be the objective of both the story and the Seller.

LAW OF CREDIBILITY

Don't say anything you can't prove.
Be ready to prove everything you say.

Denial River

During our courses, many times our attendees have discovered truthful, compelling, even unique differences from their competition, but the salespeople and managers refuse to build a story around their own discovery because it makes them uncomfortable; it goes against their sense of tradition. "This just doesn't sound right to us. We have never done it this way. That isn't the way we approach things in our industry."

It is quite common to see a company turn and walk away from its strengths and uniqueness, preferring to sound exactly like the competition because it feels comfortable. Like much in the corporate world, this defies logic, but tradition and "sounding professional" seem to be more important in management's mind than a compelling selling story. Standing arm-in-arm with the peer group seems more important than winning new business at higher-than-market fees; it seems the competition is less threatening than shifting one's internal point of view over to the Buyer's. Companies espouse "Buyer focus" but their point of view never actually changes. They continue to sell and market the same old way: "The Glories of Us and Our Magical Processes."

Without realizing it, they have become prisoners of conventional wisdom. How did the selling activity, so filled with incompetence and predictability, develop traditions that prevent experimentation with different approaches?

As we said before, some expensive cultural, organizational, and personal illusions get in the way of change.

Among those illusions:

- Buyers are really interested in how we do this.

- Buyers make their buying decisions based on relationships.

- One must have a relationship before one can sell anything.

- Our sales, marketing department, or advertising agency handles that.

- No one is going to pay more than the market price.

To retool a selling message:

- Eliminate puffery.

- Develop representations.

- Quantify benefits.

- Develop proof statements.

- Research, gather and consolidate history.

- Find unique benefits.

- Build Buyer's business context.

- Design a value position.

- Develop three important points to sell.

- Develop an ROI on your services.

Reality Check: The Executive's Five Questions

Ask your salespeople to answer the Executive's Five Questions. Then check off their answers in the predictable answer list that follows. If their presentation is mirrored in the list, then their predictability is showing.

1. Why should I spend my time talking to you?

2. Why should I buy from you rather than your competitor?

3. What makes you different from them?"

4. Why should I pay you more when they charge less?

5. Why should I switch from the service provider I know?

The Seller's Predictable Answers

We have the lowest price.

Our new software works great.

We hold the patent on the _____.

We are the only supplier of _____ in the region.

Our service is unparalleled because we listen to our customers.

We build relationships and partner with our clients.

We have a terrific buyer list.

We are the number one_____ dealer in the Southland.

We've been in business for _____ years.

We know your business.

We are the best source for_____.

We bring you the latest innovations and state-of-the-art service.

Our business slogan is "On time—On budget—Every time."

Our stuff is guaranteed.

Our most important asset is our people.

We have 20 offices to serve you.

We are a global firm.

We want your business.

The Answers Executives Look and Listen For

1. Your value position with the quantifiable benefits you offer.

2. The three key points you want the Buyer to remember.

3. Your compelling competitive advantage.

4. The three specific quantifiable benefits that prove your value.

5. Three questions that make the Buyer think about the shortcomings of what they are doing now.

Explain and quantify how your services impact your Buyer's business.

How does what you sell:

- Impact the Buyer's revenue stream?

- Impact the Buyer's expenses?

- Increase the Buyer's profitability?

- Help the Buyer reduce or manage risk?

Chapter 10—Plain Speak

"Jargon, in its most common sense, means distinctive words or phrases, used in a particular profession, trade, science, occupation, or other pursuit. Such language really amounts to specialized clichés...gibberish."

— New York Times Manual of Style and Usage

The ultimate arrogance is expecting your Buyers to understand your arcane technical language while you refuse to communicate in theirs.

Jargon and acronyms are the refuge of the lazy and the insecure. We have been trained by our culture to exaggerate, to shout, to wave our arms, to jump into the air for attention, to sound cool by using words people don't understand. No profession, no industry, no company, no manager, no salesperson is immune to the lavish use of jargon and acronyms.

Jargon slows the transfer of information and confuses the presentation. We have seen professionals so enmeshed in their industry jargon and acronyms that no Buyer could translate what they were saying. In the classroom, while trying to decode jargon, that is, agree on the meanings, the discussions often dissolve into angry arguments between professionals about the true meanings of the words they themselves invented. At the risk of sounding rhetorical, if professionals can't agree on what their jargon means, how can the Buyer be expected to understand?

While jargon lets the Seller feel more secure, or even superior, the Buyer prefers plain language. There are two million English words in use. Shakespeare used 30,000. If you want to be quickly understood, you get to use 800.

For your Buyer's sake, let the hot air out of your presentation; it is a great start toward a simple, honest, provable story that builds trust with your Buyer and sets you apart from the competition.

The experts most respected are those who can translate complex processes into simple stories.

Jargon includes acronyms, sets of initials that pretend to be so important they are known *only* by their initials, like AKC (Acronyms Kill Communication).

Cut the jargon and replace it with plain language understandable by a seventh-grader; information transmission is fastest at that level. You can do your company and your Buyers a big favor. Add your professional, business, and industry jargon to the black hole list.

Chapter 11—Your Fee

To avoid cutting your price and to preserve your profits, learn to answer the price objection well. The time and agony spent developing answers will be returned a hundredfold. (And this isn't puffery either.)

The only real price objections:

- I don't have the money.
- I don't believe your stuff is worth the money.

You can't do much about the first objection if you can't arrange financing.

It is the second fee objection that kills. This is where the content-free story gets expensive; it creates its own competition; it encourages the Buyer to call up your competitors for a chat.

Most sellers are held captive inside the stamping, snorting herd of their competitors because they puff. Over time, said competitive herd becomes referred to as "The Industry" and accepted wisdom, customs, and pricing become "The Market"—both euphemisms for the word "Competitors."

Studies show that the Buyer makes decisions based on the following priorities in this order: confidence, quality, selection, service, and (fifth and last) price.

When puffery makes all firms sound alike, the Buyer has nothing by which to judge relative value, so price is left as the only decision making criterion.

Like a fisherman, the Buyer's role is to catch the biggest fish with the smallest hook, and Buyers use competitive quotes as bait.[12]

From past experience, the Buyer has learned that the Seller is defenseless and that any fee quoted can be reduced to the market price. Upon hearing the fee quoted, all the Buyer has to do is deliver a hard stare and a snort of derision.

The predictable response from the Seller is, "Now wait! This isn't carved in stone... we can talk about this... your business is important to us... let's see what we can do here... this is just the starting point!"

When the Buyer forces the Seller to focus on price alone, stripped of all the offsetting benefits that justify it, then the Seller must take what is offered. However, it is often the Seller, not the Buyer, who makes the fee the controlling issue. The first rule of price negotiation is never negotiate price by itself. Defending your fee without offsetting quantified benefits is a fool's errand. There is no contest. You will lose.

FEE-VALUE RULE

Never quote a fee—which is a feature—
without benefits that justify the value.

To defend your asking price, you must advance compelling, quantified benefits that are the counterweight to your heavy fee. You have no choice: no benefits, no counterweight.

The price objection is about numbers; thus your answer must be about numbers. This is the point in your presentation where the preparation of quantified benefits pays off.

The simplest way to get a higher price is to:

- Impact the Buyer's revenue stream; help the Buyer convert his products and services into cash.

- Convert liabilities into assets.

- Change your fees into investments with an ROI.

- Help reduce the prospect's costs or risks. (Save time, effort, money; manage risk; etc.)

- Help increase the Buyer's profits. (Create dividends, cash, cash flow, market share, total value, etc.)

The Level Playing Field

Without a selling proposition in the Buyer's terms, Sellers must rely on getting their fair share of the available business.

In today's business environment, the concept of settling for a fair share or playing on a level field is ludicrous. If a professional settles for a fair share of the market, he will simply become a stepping-stone for those ambitious folk who refuse to settle.

The Buyer uses the market, that is, the competitor's information, to seize control of the transaction, create a level playing field, and neutralize the Seller's negotiating advantage. The embarrassing part is how easy the Seller makes it for the Buyer.

We teach some of the world's most highly trained professional services consultants. They have world-class reputations, client lists, and histories. The results they deliver are breathtaking. However, they have little sense of the value of their work in the Client's world, so they are unprepared to set fees commensurate with the spectacular results they deliver. Therefore they are perceived as a commodity and they are reduced to being paid as hourly workers, professional field hands, rather than the creative, highly trained service providers they really are.

With a Buyer's story, it is not only possible but likely that a Seller can tilt the playing field and gain more than its fair share of business.

• •

One of our students, a consulting partner said he had "done well" for a recent Client and was immediately challenged.

"How well?" a partner asked.

He stepped outside the room, called the Client and reported back. "Forty-five million. Our service made their company 45 million dollars."

"What was our fee for that engagement?" another asked.

"Seventy-five thousand."

The partners groaned in unison.

• •

LAW OF PRICE

If you can't explain in words why your stuff
is worth your asking price, then it isn't.

Chapter 12—Why should I spend my time talking to you?

This question cuts through the doughy fat layers into the muscle tissue of your business. If you can answer this question from the Buyer's point of view, you know what you do for a living. If you can't, you don't.

This is your first (and perhaps only) opportunity to tell your story to a potential Buyer. It is the lead paragraph in your business story and speaks directly to the Buyer's business context, implies or directly addresses the Buyer's business or personal loss or gain; it signals the Buyer that there is an objective to the meeting, that the conversation is going to be about his business, not your stuff.

Your lead, the **value position,** is used as part of your introduction, your opening line in a cold call, or whenever you are asked about your business. It should contain a compelling reason for the Buyer to buy from you, a central theme, or the strongest benefit you bring to the Buyer. It is the scene-setter for your conversation. Done well, this statement seizes the Buyer's full attention. (Don't confuse the value position for the Buyer with your broader, more complex, and usually self-serving internal company vision or mission statement.)

Here are some examples of value positions:

- FrontWheel Corporate Services provides facility asset management that can help you reallocate maintenance spending and reduce your capital requirements by as much as 30%.

- A quarter of all companies fail to realize any benefits of a business acquisition during the first two years. Pinstrype Consulting's Accelerated Profit process reduces merger transition time by 75%.

- Acme Law Firm's compliance reviews uncover plan defects before they can cause IRS fines that can be as much as 25% of plan assets.

The examples above show you a road map of how to design your own value positions. They are not actual; you get to plug in your own stuff.

Here are some real ones:

- We help establish profitable, sustainable U.S. operations for select European consumer goods companies. Kastel's clients have more than doubled their existing U.S. businesses within 1 to 2 years, or established profitable new businesses within 12 months.

- Fifteen minutes with Geico could save you 15% on your car insurance.

- Bain & Company is a global business consulting firm. Our business is helping to make companies more valuable. Our clients have historically outperformed the stock market by 4:1.

- VASS® retrains companies that must sell at the executive level to grow their revenues 25% to 100%.

SELLING IS TRADING

You trade benefits for everything you want from the Buyer—time, attention, appointments, fees, trust, loyalty.

Features are not trading stock.

From a Buyer's point of view, nothing substantive happens (you have nothing to trade) until the dialogue arrives at the benefits. Knowing that, why not start with your trading stock—benefits— rather than waste a whole bunch of time talking about stuff that the Buyer neither cares about nor hears.

Decode Your Value

You are in business to solve problems for your Buyers; they are interested in your business solely for what's in it for them. Answer these positioning questions about the relationship between your service and your Buyer:

- When you solve the Buyer's problems, what benefits do your solutions bring to them?

- What business and personal problems do you solve for your Buyer?

- How are your Buyers diminished without your services?

- What risks of loss do they have?

- How are they hassled, overworked, underpaid, under-loved, under-serviced, anxious, afraid, broke, depressed, etc?

- How do you make Buyers a profit, or save time, hassle, money or man-hours? Give power?

Increase market share? Increase self-esteem? Make more desirable? Help image? Prevent losses, Reduce risk, etc?

- To some degree, all of us compete in a hostile environment. When compared to your strongest competitors, what features, advantages, and the resulting benefits of your firm are superior or unique?

- What is your firm's competitive advantage?

- Usual benefits are power, profit, prestige, or pleasure. For the executive, add time, money, and risk. How do you quantify and prove your benefits?

LAW OF CLARITY

If you can't explain what you sell to a 10-year-old in words he can understand, then you don't know what you sell.[13]

Chapter 13—Why should I hire you rather than your competitor?

In a persuasive conversation, the executive Buyer can only remember three points.

What three points will you use? (We recommend your best advantage—how you deliver your service—and two benefits: ROI and the time required to recoup the fee or costs.)

Using a consulting business as an example:

- We see our process as a single service with a dozen different disciplines. We help you avoid the inherent risks of liabilities that can occur when you use different, uncoordinated firms for each discipline.

- Our clients report a three- to five-times return on our fee within one year through new operational efficiencies and avoided losses.

- Our clients have found they usually recover our fee within 45 days by saving the fees they would have paid for redundant services.

Decode Your Benefits

- How do your services save the Buyer money?

- How do your services create money for the Buyer?

- What dire business consequences have befallen other Buyers who didn't use your service?

- What provable benefits is the Buyer doing without if she is not using your service that directly impacts her life? Impacts her firm's survival, profit or cash flow?

CHAPTER 14—WHAT MAKES YOU DIFFERENT FROM THEM?

Here is where differentiation kicks in. What is your firm's sustainable, differentiating, or compelling competitive advantage expressed in the Buyer's terms?

Not taking a selling position *is* a taking a position. If you do not position yourself, your competition will do it for you. Competitors love voids because it is easier to falsely characterize you and your firm's services. And since you have no selling position, the contest turns into a schoolyard-style confrontation: "No, we don't—Yes, you do—No, we don't—Yes, you do."

A sales presentation cannot be repositioned without decoding stuff and process, that is, features and advantages, into benefits for the Buyer. Only with quantifiable benefits can a firm express its uniqueness. Analyze your firm's strengths and use them to isolate and quantify a unique benefit.

Since the Buyer perceives features to be interchangeable, "commoditized" by competition, it is no longer enough to produce a zero-defect product or service. Many companies come very close to zero defects and still can't differentiate

their stuff. Nowadays, it's how you sell your stuff—
how well you migrate to the Buyer's point of view
when telling a story—that will differentiate you.

Genuine long-term differentiation is generated as
much by how you and your firm handle the Buyer
as it is by the benefits of the product or service
itself. Sometimes more.

Decode Your Uniqueness

What unique information and quantified benefits
will help the executive Buyer choose your firm as
the best solution to his problem?

Chapter 15—Why should I pay you more when they charge less?

Three quantifiable benefits are required here, benefits like ROI, time to recoup your fee, dollars saved, risks mitigated, etc.

By determining the monetary results your firm has created for past Buyers, you can project an average return on the Buyer's investment in your services. (The Buyer isn't looking for an exact number; he is looking for context.)

More and more, Buyers are no longer settling for BS stories. They want numbers; they want professional service providers to justify their fees in dollars and cents. The Buyer's demanding attitude is resented by Sellers who worked so hard to earn a credential and learn a profession that did not have to account for themselves beyond "I have credentials and that should be enough." That was then; this is now.

• •

You go shopping for a new car. You tell the salesman, "I want to look at cars."

The salesman says, "That won't be necessary. Write me a check for $40,000 and I'll pick one out for you."

You say, "Wait a minute, how do I know what I'm buying? How do I know I'll like it?"

"Because I am a professional and I know what you want. I'm a graduate of the Peoria Automotive Institute with a WFO, CYA, and a BFD in car science and you're not. You can trust me."

• •

This is the way most professionals sell, yet they are surprised when the Buyer balks.

The more benefits you sell (the more trading stock) the more likely you are to get your asking price. The more features you sell the more likely you are to have your competitor set the price for you.

An example of three benefits:

- Our job is to reduce your risk by 75% in this transaction.

- Based on what our other Buyers tell us, you may expect an ROI of three to five times our fee for this matter.

- Historically, our fee can be returned to you within 60 days due to the results we normally achieve in these transactions.

Decode Your ROI

What specific quantifiable benefits will you
use to prove your value to the executive Buyer?
(Remember, the Buyer can remember only three.)

CHAPTER 16—WHY SHOULD I SWITCH FROM THE SERVICE PROVIDER I KNOW?

Because change is so difficult and expensive, especially changing consultants, most Buyers are pretty happy to continue doing what they do now and rehire the same people they use now. Buyers love the status quo; it is a fact of life. Paradoxically they also like to make changes just for the sake of change. For instance, in the advertising agency business, even though the advertising may be pulling well, many times clients change agencies just because they tire of the same faces, same account execs with the same jokes, and the same advertising "look."

The idea that a competitor has serviced a client for years and, therefore, the competitor "owns" that client, is silly rationalization for not calling on a Buyer. If your story is compelling and different, potential Buyers want to talk to you. They want to know what you know. However, if your message is "me too," why should they waste their time? And why should you?

There are only two choices with a status quo Buyer:

1. Leave.
2. Ask questions that require that the Buyer think differently to answer intelligently. The

questions that create a different frame of reference that allows them to discover the shortcomings of what they are doing now.

Here are some examples of questions that change a Buyer's frame of reference:

- How are you going about defending yourself with only 16% of the available information?

- How do you protect your profits from the discounters?

- How are you going about protecting your reputation in the financial community?

- How are you protecting the company from the risk of a huge verdict in a bad jurisdiction?

- How do you avoid paying for redundant work?

Careful thought is required to design the questions that revolve around what the Buyer *lacks* with what he is doing now. It is probing around the hole in the doughnut. By asking about your competition's services or the Buyer's "I'll do it myself" stance, usually the hole will be revealed. Until a hole is found, trying to get hired by someone who is satisfied is a waste of time. Designing questions a Buyer will freely answer is explored more fully in our book *Soft Selling in a Hard World* available at www.amazon.com.

The idea is to open a conversation with questions that require the Buyer to think carefully about the answer. If the Buyer's initial reaction is "Huh?" you are probably on the right track. They need time to digest the implications of intelligent questions (which they are not used to hearing.)

Decode Your Questions

What three questions will you ask to lead the Buyer into a Persuasive Executive Conversation?

CHAPTER 17—PROOF STATEMENTS

In customer surveys the sellers ask in one form or another, "How did we do?" The correct question is, "How did you do?" By changing the point of view of the survey to determine the clients' results, valuable proof statements can be collected and your firm can learn what their client's real story is about.

So where does one come by quantified benefits? From your own files; from your history with past engagements; from your Clients. Phone them. Ask them. While they may not give you an exact number, they can usually give you a range. Ensure that your salespeople call clients back after they use your services to check on the results your stuff created for them. (We have a Client that will not give salespeople their commission check until quantified results from the Client are obtained.)

After you have gathered a number of these, say twenty or so, you will see a pattern of results. From that pattern you can then develop a range of benefits, for instance: "9% to 21%" on your stuff. (A range of results is okay. The Buyer is looking for an idea of what he might expect to gain. Don't get hung up on determining a single result.)

• •

Since no manager in his right mind would hire a training firm without a trial course, we delivered a test program to a large (very large) consulting firm. The attendees were all heavily degreed folks with huge expertise and experience. The first day we insisted that they give us some sense of magnitude, an idea of what they were worth to their Buyers in dollars and cents.

They hated the concept. And they were very angry at us; they felt we didn't understand their business; our instructions didn't apply to their professional services; there was no possible way to derive these metrics. At day's end, they held a meeting to determine if they would fire us or allow us to complete our three-day program.

After an hour of heated argument, a senior partner said, "We say we are world experts in our field. Isn't it embarrassing that we don't know these answers. Maybe we should try to quantify some of our results."

Over the next two hours, they brainstormed and isolated 200 possibilities but agreed that it would take too much time to research them all so a list of 25 were isolated to be quantified. A partner was taken offline for a month to do the research so each could be proven.

The first sale after research was 11 million dollars using just three provable benefits.

● ●

Disraeli said "There are lies, damned lies and statistics." Remember to be ready to prove everything you say.

Chapter 18—Prepare the Persuasive Executive Conversation

It is possible (rather easy actually) to build your entire conversation on benefits without features being mentioned, especially with complex services. The higher your level of contact in the organization the more benefits you may discuss and the more features you may avoid. At the CEO level, it's all quantifiable benefits. If your executive-level Buyer wants to talk about features he'll let you know. He's a big boy. If he doesn't ask, don't tell.

Your story is like a movie. It must be logical and understandable, and its message, both context and subtext, quickly transmitted.

Speak in the Buyer's context and language.

- Tell the interesting 10% of your story. Present in five minutes or less. Less is better.

- Be ready to solve the Buyer's business and personal problems.

- At the CEO/COO level, position your sale to impact the Buyer's survival, profit, and cash flow.

- At the middle management level, impact survival.

- Be able to pay for the changeover from the old vendor to you, the new vendor, with quantifiable benefits of your service.

LAW OF CIVILIZATION

A pitch is not a Persuasive Executive
Conversation.

Executives say

> Don't waste my time with big buildups.

> Get to the point in 10 seconds.

> Tell me the provable truth.

> Don't treat me like a "mark."

> Solve my problem and give me your solution in my language.

> If I give you a dollar for your services, how many do I get back and when?

Decode Your Selling Position

- Define your reason for being in business.

- Diagnose what you sell, the current market responses, competition, and trends.

- Find your competitive advantage.

- Separate puffery and representation.

- Separate features and benefits.

- Quantify benefits.

- Explain benefits as representation.

- Build your value position.

Fighting Words

"The consumer is not a moron. She is your wife. Never write an advertisement you would not want your own family to read. You would not tell lies to your wife. Don't tell them to mine."

—David Ogilvy (1911-1999)

A creative genius famous for his long ad copy, David Ogilvy was an advertising giant. He said, "Make the copy interesting, no matter how long, and people will read it." That was yesterday.

Nowadays, it is a mistake to assume that people read. Buyers do not read. That is a fact of modern life. They can read. They have been known to read in the past. They may read again someday in the future but not in your lifetime.

Writing officialese like a lawyer, banker, or government worker goes against your cause (even though parents spend thousand of dollars sending their kids to college to master the arcane arts of smoke and dust so that things seem more complex than they really are).

Keep your writing simple. Abhor obfuscation. Clear writing indicates clear thinking, an enviable attribute in business.

If you want to get read, you will be way ahead of the game if you assume that nobody in the world will *ever* read the deathless prose you write about your business. Inquiring minds want to know in one short sentence. Which means keep it short, keep it tight, keep it light, keep it simple. A flood of information drowns the readers attention.

Chapter 19—Marketing Magic

Business Mysteries

If management can take all the credit for leading a company into the bright light of profit, it must take all the blame for keeping Buyers in the dark.

Cumulative error begins when management assigns sales positioning and decision making to the marketing department and the ad agency with the assumption that those people know what they are doing. As you can see when you visit company web sites, these are lousy assumptions.

The ambition of nearly every management board is to expand its influence in ever-widening circles to eventually control the market.

So the marketing department conspires with the ad agency to assemble a marketing approach that will accomplish management's grand plan to rule the world. Management works for the shareholders (in theory anyway). It sends guidance down to the marketing and sales department impressing upon them how important it is to make this year's numbers.

To that end, management commands the marketing and sales department to go out in the world and spread the gospel offering the "highest quality" and "best of breed," both being indefensible market positions as both are puffery.

In the "big marketing meeting," everybody huddles and begins to bounce ideas around on how to do management's bidding. So the discussion is thrown off-center from the start. Everyone looks to the middle of the conference table, turns inward, and discusses the processes, the features, and advantages of their stuff.

They discuss and labor mightily to bring forth a tricky and expensive ad campaign to expand their hegemony. And right here is the essence of the problem: They take in each others' laundry, smoke their own exhaust, and believe their own myths based on the three fraudulent assumptions noted earlier.

- Everybody cares about our stuff.

- If Buyers knew the technical stuff we know, they would see how good we are.

- Buyers will believe us because we are DifferentBiz, Inc., a global company that specializes in everything for everybody, 24/7/365.

Conventional wisdom says that the reason a company exists is to create profits for the stockholders. From the Buyer's point of view, the only reason a firm exists is to create a profit for them, the Buyer. In the Buyer's mind, a firm does not exist for any other reason.

Management worries about the stockholders and forgets that in order to get stockholders what they want, it is management's job to first get Buyers what they want: the ball has to bounce, first to the Buyer's profit needs and *then* to the stockholders.

Marketers aim at the wrong target: Management's demands. The correct aiming point for the big marketing meeting is fulfillment of the Buyer's needs expressed as quantifiable business benefits:

- How can we make our Buyers 5% more profit?

- How can we help them sell more software, soft drinks, real estate, insurance, cleaning services, etc.?

- How can we add to their bottom line?

- How can we save them time and money? How much, based on our history?

- What risks are they facing?

- What is the magnitude of those risks?

- How can we help them manage or reduce those risks?

Remove Buyers from the business equation and you have no business. Obvious, right? If this is so obvious, why do companies keep secret what they do for a living? Because management says, "We have great stuff!" What the Buyer needs, believes, and wants to know gets lost.

How does something as obvious as the story for the Buyer get overlooked?

The answer is life: the day-to-day rattle and battle of the marketplace. Often there is little time or a suitable venue, and little desire for tangling with sticky marketing issues like positioning the firm in the marketplace. (The idea of positioning, like tennis, is to hit the ball where the competitor isn't.)

Buyers are no help; they have their own problems. They aren't going to criticize the Seller's marketing program wherein the Seller talks a private, jargon-filled language. The Buyer's default reactions are, "That's nice." or "We already have people who do that." or "No, thank you." or "Your fee is too high."

With management's direct participation, the entire firm ought to sit facing away from the center of the table discussing the only thing that is important: the Buyer's world, his money, his ambitions, his creativity, his problems, his survival, profit and cash flow. There should be a person in the room who plays the cynical Buyer who is totally apathetic about the glories of the firm. His job is to ask at every step, "What's in it for me?"

Whether they admit it or not everyone has competition. It may not be direct competition but the Buyer has limited resources—money, time, and attention—so everyone is competing for those limited resources.

In marketing, time is the enemy. While the competition for the Buyer's attention has multiplied a thousandfold since 1900, his or her time on the earth has increased by only 60%. No matter how hard one tries, neither time nor Buyer's attention is elastic. The Buyer's attention must be bought with benefits.

Why isn't there a "Buyer's rep" included? The reason is "groupthink," a condition where one becomes an outcast by disagreeing with an idea accepted among peers.

"We are good," the leader says, "perhaps the best in our industry."

To which the Buyer's rep says, "That's BS. You sound just like the competition."

Sellers spend their time convincing themselves of the high value they contribute to their company rather than the value they bring to their Buyers. They do not enjoy hearing about their shortcomings from internal skeptics. Criticism by the skeptic is written off with "That guy just doesn't get it."

● ●

During a training meeting, partners of a large consulting firm had the opportunity to role-play their sales presentation to an outsider acting as their Buyer.

The presentations did not go well. As the consultants pitched their stuff, the Buyer insisted on knowing what was in it for him and his business.

Afterwards, the partners complained that the Buyer was not a competent or educated Buyer; he did not know enough about business to play his role correctly.

The Buyer was the former CEO of a Fortune 1000 company.

● ●

Techies love their computer stuff and that new invention, the Internet. They forget, or don't know, that they need to produce a quantifiable solution to a real problem and translate that into the Buyer's language. (It is a given that we Buyers always lag behind the bleeding edge of technology and rarely know the arcane language that is added daily by tech folks.)

In an example writ large, dot-coms confused their processes with the results they could deliver to their Buyers. Investors did, too; they bought into rafts of technical information presented as a "business" model by the venture capitalists and stockbrokers. They were not business models. A real business model calls for results in the form of profits and quantifiable benefits generated for the Buyer, not processes and stuff.

Had everyone in the business chain from entrepreneur to stockbroker been required to develop a Buyer's story, hundreds of millions in capital losses would have been avoided because most of the dot-coms had no real business plan and would never have been funded.

Most of the dot-coms solved problems nobody had—they left their Buyers' profits completely out of the business equation. They went broke because they deserved to.

The Brand

My father, a ham-handed ex-prizefighter, construction boss, and martinet, used to say, "The easiest thing to find is someone who tells you they can do the work. The hardest thing to find is someone who actually does the work."

The way to build your brand and your firm is to under-promise and over-deliver. If branding is your goal, develop a story that promises the Buyer benefits and then deliver perfectly on the promise.

Creating a respected brand, that is, developing brand equity, is the result of a firm's actions for its Clients. Millions are spent on branding campaigns that create little brand equity because the advertised service doesn't fulfill the implied promise of the brand. If performance is missing, the brand is just window dressing, a movie set.

If your firm does the work, you become a valuable tool for your clients and they will love and protect you. They will sell you inside their organizations and to strangers at the Martini bar. They actually become your upbeat, unpaid sales force. If your clients aren't selling for you then you probably aren't doing the work and, for you, exotic concepts like branding are moot.

Reality Check: Decode Your Collateral Materials

Since features, advantages, and benefits have been their life's work all the way back to Marketing 101, your marketing department can go into shock over this test.

Take a look at your company's advertising literature, videos, brochures, proposals, annual reports, product data sheets, PR releases, web site, etc. Use a **blue** marker to highlight the puffery, opinion, the subjective and unproved claims, black-hole words, and jargon.

Then use a **yellow** marker to highlight each feature—your stuff. With a **green** marker highlight each benefit—the Buyer's stuff. Ideally the ratio of features to benefits should be 1:1. A ratio of less than 3:1 means you are wasting time and money. We see many that are 30:1, or more. Most have no benefits whatsoever.

Once you become sensitized to the difference between your stuff and the Buyer's stuff, you will see this confusion everywhere you turn: billboards, trade shows, advertising, collateral material, company slogans, your own presentations. At first you may see the differences as subtle. Then they become obvious, then dramatic. And then appalling.

Design Wars

Inside many organizations rages an ongoing war between the designers of the stuff and the sellers of the stuff. And it causes confusion.

When sales are down, managers spend their attention developing "new and improved" stuff. They concentrate on priming salespeople with ever-more-technical information. Encouraged (or threatened) by management, the salesperson ends up selling the wrong stuff: features.

The designers of the stuff insist that when the Buyer sees their marvelous new features, then he will be so blown away that the product or service will sell itself. When the Buyer yawns at the latest whiz-bang feature, the seller reports the Buyer's indifference to management. The manager says, "Did you tell them about our new software that separates the clurd from the durd?"

Seller says, "Yep. And they didn't care."

Manager says, "Well, did you tell 'em that it also plays CDs, MP3s, baby-sits their kids, shows classic movies, analyzes business plans, accurately predicts the weather, and automatically invests only in winning stocks?"

"Yep. Buyer said they all do that."

"Yeah, but not with a clurd-durd separator *built right in!*"

Managers force salespeople to become professionals in the features yet remain amateurs at benefits. When the features remain un-translated into benefits, even the hottest new feature becomes commoditized and pricing power is lost. Even if the Buyer thinks your features are great, he can't connect it to his world, his problem, or his personal life. No benefits equals no context for the Buyer.

● ●

My daughter, a video writer-producer created many promotional videos for a huge high-tech company. She knew the difference between features and benefits. In the natural flow of writing scripts to promote various products and services, she always scripted benefits for the Buyer to complement the features. Before shooting, the benefits were deleted by the marketers. In every case, not one benefit ever lit the video screen.

● ●

The way to *commoditize* your new feature is to sell the feature. The way to *capitalize* your new feature is to decode the features and translate them into benefits.

Reality Check: Decode Your Client Meetings

Ask your people how they organize their presentations. This is generally greeted with blank stares or a three-part plan, that when reduced to its elements, is a permutation of "Build a relationship," then "All about us," and then, "What do you think about us?"

Diagram of a typical pitch:

Have your people deliver a presentation in the words they actually use. Have them role-play with you as the Buyer. Be sure they stay in their first-person role rather than revert to "This is what I would say."

What to listen for:

- How many puffery phrases—unproved claims—were used?

- What truthful representations were used?

- How many black-hole words were used?

- How much industry or professional jargon was used?

- What were the Buyer's business (not stuff) problems?

- What were the solutions suggested to solve the Buyer's business problems?

- What was said that gave the Buyer a sense of magnitude of the benefits offered?

- Did they tell only the interesting 10% of their story?

- Did they get to the point in 10 seconds or less?

- Did they present fully in five minutes or less?

- Did they position their sale to impact the Buyer's survival, profit, and cash flow?

- Did they justify their fee with quantifiable benefits?

- What questions did they ask to get hired?

Keepers of Secrets

Due to the holes in their presentation, salespeople keep secret:

- How their stuff works within the Buyer's business

- What business they are really in from the Buyer's point of view

- Their unique selling proposition or competitive advantage

- How their service is different from the competition

- What results in time, money, and risk their service delivers to the Buyer

- Why their product or service is worth the asking price

Chapter 20—Presentations to Boards

When selling to groups, answering a request for proposal, going head-to-head with your toughest "short-list" competitors, or delivering a boardroom presentation, salespeople and managers alike approach these presentations the same way a guy in plaid pants, plaid shirt, and plaid tie approaches a woman in a singles bar: he introduces himself, does 45 minutes on the "Glories of Me" and, catching himself over-talking, decides to involve the woman in this adventure. So bending close, he peers deeply into her eyes and speaks in a confidential half-whisper, "Well, enough about me. What do you think about me?"

On every point to be raised in the big executive meeting, ask this question: "Is this for the Buyer or is this for us?" If the points are for you, they are features. If they are for the Buyer in some form of power, profit, prestige, or pleasure: time, money, and risk, then they are benefits.

Millions of hours and dollars are spent on PowerPoint® slides, graphic art, photography, writing, editors, advertising talent, consultants, rehearsals, projection equipment, and electricity all to present exactly like the plaid doofus in the singles bar.

We work with reputable and well-known firms with large brand equity that expend much of their selling capital talking to their Buyers about the credentials of the firm when the credentials are the very reason they were invited in the first place. It is a waste of the Buyer's valuable time. Plus, it focuses the discussion on the Seller's stuff rather than on the Buyer's situation. Illustrious history and the company's heroes, which are features, are rarely (read: never) tied to a benefit for the Buyer.

The culture and conventional wisdom have trained Buyers to expect a five-step show-and-tell presentation:

1. Make the introduction.

2. Vomit the "Glories of Us" using as much time as the Buyer will allow.

3. Give a polite "Thanks for allowing us to present our stuff."

4. Split to the nearest watering hole to discuss how hot the graphics and charts looked. "Boy, we walked right in there and knocked 'em dead, didn't we? Dang, are we good or what!"

5. Wait for the phone call.

When you allow the way it's always been done or "this is what they expect" to dictate how and what you present, then you set an exquisite trap for your company and its salespeople.

Traditional group presentations are big on show business and small on memorable material. Just the opposite is ideal: solid on recall and transparent on show business.

Sellers often assume that this is just another presentation of their stuff and assume Buyers are just looking and unready to make a real decision; this is a self-imposed limitation. Our experience shows that Buyers are often more than ready.

We have several clients whose business growth relies entirely on winning short-list presentations, that is, "beauty contests" against their best competitors. By changing their format from a features-oriented pitch to a benefits-driven discussion about the Buyer's problems, they have increased their success rate fivefold.

The challenge is to stop talking about the "Glories of Us" and our stuff and to discuss the Buyer's problems, the potential solutions, and the benefits of the solutions that reward the Buyer's committee for spending time with you. (Trading stock, remember?)

• •

I learned an important entrepreneurial lesson from a good ol' boy from south Texas who had been a national-class motorcycle racer. The replacement parts in his body set off airport metal detectors. I was his adoring student. We slowly walked the motocross track, heads down, kicking clods, studying this turn and that berm, and discussing the tactics of using each rutted feature for the fastest line. Way out on the backside of the course, he stopped and rubbed his alloy elbow, his eyes focused far off, out across the snaky dirt track, across the adobe hills of western Colorado.

"Just remember," he said, "you can do everything exactly right and still lose. To win, you can't follow the rider ahead of you because the best you can finish is second. You gotta pick your own line and ride your own race."

• •

To guarantee that your appearance will be quickly forgotten, give the traditional five-step show-and-tell presentation. To be remembered, set your mind to "ride your own race" and create a presentation that differentiates you. The usual feature-filled, benefits-empty "All about Us" monologue is boring, predictable, and wholly forgettable.

• •

Once upon a time, I was engaged to help IBM's professional presenters reformat the presentations they gave to their very largest customers. To prepare for the assignment, I observed their typical presentation.

In front of each attendee was placed a written agenda. The 8:30 A.M. event was "History of IBM." The next event began at 10:30 A.M. It was two hours of more than you ever wanted to know about Big Blue.

Agony.

Working with the presenters, we decoded those first two hours of boring lecture and slides. The IBM history became: "Today's IBM was started in 1924. We invented the first commercially successful general purpose computer. We are 10 times bigger than our nearest competitor." The history of IBM in six seconds.

• •

Of course, in this case the history dissertation was moot. Who doesn't know this firm and what it does? Why tell everybody again? One doesn't look at the sun every morning and exclaim, "Well, the sun came up again today. What a surprise!" Many mainline companies waste the Buyer's time like this.

If your firm has good brand equity or is well known in your industry, why mention the firm's history at all?

History has little to do with the Buyer. The Buyer is thinking, "I know IBM. What does this history have to do with the $39-million problem in my IT department?"

There are four problems in presenting to groups of Buyers:

- The number of competitors that are presenting against you

- The predictable and boring show-and-tell, everyone-sounds-alike nature of traditional presentations

- The transitory nature of your glory—your Buyers will remember only 10% or less of what you present after one week

- You may be just a due diligence player for a decision that has already been made

Few salespeople have looked critically at the reasons they got awarded business. They chalk it up to "We have a great relationship." or "We had the best stuff." or "We made a great presentation!" which is usually not the case.

Chapter 21—The Afternoon Movie

With PowerPoint®, you *can* make a movie but that doesn't mean you *should* make a movie. Executives hate PowerPoint®; 40% admit to falling asleep during these tedious presentations. A lighted screen is a conversation killer; therefore, the entire slide presentation should last no longer than a couple of minutes.

While we have clients who insist on using slides, we have reduced their 50-to-250 slide "decks" that explained "The Glories of Us" to a merciful six or seven simple graphics. The Executive's Five Questions can be answered in five slides. Add a disclaimer; that's six. Add a 25-word overview of the company history or philosophy or reputation ("The Glories of Us"); that's seven.

Some of our clients have been hired at their first interview using a single sheet of paper. A number have found that a simple place-mat containing the salient information works well, too, avoiding inherently boring slides altogether.

Reality Check: Competitive Presentations

In a one-hour presentation, how many minutes do your people talk? (It should be an open-ended conversation based on Q&A. The Sellers should talk no more than 40% of the time.)

- How many PowerPoint® slides are used? (Ten maximum.)

- How many people on your presentations team? (Three maximum.)

- What is the stated objective for the meeting? (To get hired in the room at that meeting.)

- How are you going to get hired in the meeting? (What is the first task of this assignment if you get it?)

- What three points do you make to the Buyers? (One advantage, two quantified benefits.)

Review the written material your people prepared for their last three presentations.

- What percentage of the text and graphics were Buyer benefits? (At least 50%?)

CHAPTER 22—HIGH-TECH FACE, LOW-TECH IDEA

When developing a web site to put your company in front of future customers, the project is too important to be left to the marketing department or the ad agency whose very stock in trade is puffery. It is too important to be left to web designers—computer people who know little or nothing about your message or how to design it. We have seen a number of firms that bought into the idea that the web created magic and a web designer was the magician who could design the site and the message, too. So the most important marketing function, the message, was turned over to a computer nerd who knows everything about computers and nothing about marketing. It is much like turning brain surgery over to the electrician who wired the operating room.

Reality Check: Web Site

When viewing your home page:

- Can the visitor tell what you do for them in four seconds or less?

- Is your message about the "Glories of Your Stuff" or about the Buyers' problems you have solved and the results of your solutions?

- Is your page fact-based, that is: representation or puffery?

- Is there too much crowded text to easily read?

The Message

What is the business objective of the site? To show credentials? As an online brochure? To sell your service? To steer the visitor to a live person somewhere? To close business, that is, get hired?

- Does the home page explain simply what business you are in from your Buyer's point of view, in the form of the value position of your firm?

- Is your value position simple? That is, is it under 25 words, declaratory, and straightforward?

- Can a 10-year-old understand precisely what you are saying?

- Is your lead benefit quantified?

- Is there a continuing story throughout the site? How do you impact a Buyer's business in time, money, or risk?

- Does it explain the problems you solve, your solution, and the benefits of your solution?

- Are your proof statements obvious and easily accessible?

- Do your proof statements contain benefits?

- Is it jargon-filled?

- Does it convey ideas that are easily understood by the uninformed visitor?

- What simple action can the Buyer take to buy from you?

- Is navigation simple for the visitor? Is there a telephone number and email address on the home page where the customer can talk to a live person and avoid the site altogether?

- Would you buy from this site? Have you actually tried?

The Mechanics

- Does it load quickly?

- Can you navigate throughout the site from the home page?

- Does the visitor remain oriented while deep in the site?

- Following any thread, is it more than three pages deep?

- Is the text 14 point or larger without italics, clearly and easily read?

- Is there an FAQ for the quick visitor?

- Is there a way for it to be interactive? Is there a reason? Is interactivity in line with your business objective?

- Do the mechanics resonate with the marketing message?

- Is there a contact address with phone number that is easily found on the home page?

Chapter 23—The Wrap

"To know and not to do is not to know."

—Zen

Understanding a concept is not the same as executing it. Understanding these ideas is easy. Executing these ideas is hard.

Knowing is not doing. Planning is not execution. Strategy is not tactics. Ideas are not action. To execute your new Persuasive Executive Conversation, you will take risks. Where there is risk, there is reward. The reward is that the Executive Suite will give you time to tell your story and hire you because of it. When selling at the executive level, one cannot ask for more.

The large mental and money investment you have in your current way of doing things makes absolutely no difference to the Buyer. Conventional wisdom is your problem, not theirs.

Placing your Buyer in a separate part of your business consciousness, "us" and "them," halves your effectiveness. It subtly turns your "service" organization into a "self-service" one and few things are more obvious to sophisticated Buyers. Little remains hidden from them if you act only in your self-interest.

The game is yours when, alone in the dark of night, you ask yourself the straight, unvarnished, critical question: "Is my Buyer or Client better off for doing business with me?" and your answer is an honest "Yes."

Magic Bullet

"It's not what you don't know that hurts you. It's what you think you know that ain't so."

—Will Rogers

This isn't everything you need to know about selling into the executive suite. Being in the right place at the right time plays a big part of good business. Of course, there are always those cornball clichés that the harder you work the luckier you get and luck is the meeting of preparation and opportunity and all that jazz. The more you risks you take, the more you exercise your selling muscles, the better your chances of being in the right place at the right time.

Salespeople are always looking for the magic bullet: the one idea that puts them in total control of every situation and allows them to close every transaction. There is no magic bullet. We don't have it and no one else does either. In sales, nothing works all the time; anyone who writes about closing every transaction is not a salesperson: he is either an order-taker, a prevaricator, or a dreamer.

In behavior modification, which good training is, we apply the 80% rule. If something works 80% of the time, that is as good as life gets. You can strive for perfection but don't expect it; the 80%, however, will get you more money than you can spend.

A bit of flag waving: I have lived the American dream. Starting poor, I never had to ask for permission to succeed or fail; the door of opportunity was always open; all I had to do was take the risk and walk through it. In America, to remain unsuccessful is a choice because the door is open to everyone. Not every door is open to every citizen equally. But there is enough of a crack that each of us can better our lot in life if we take the risk of walking through it and work for, and expect, success.

Here's the message: Whatever you think your limitation is, that is your limitation. In America, you don't have to ask for permission.

Good luck and good hunting. Sell well—live well.

Jerry Vass

••••••••••••••••••••••••••••••••••••

The Strategy King

Once upon a time in a far-off land, the King gathered around him his most trusted subjects. Smiling beneficently, he spoke thus: "You are all sidewalk knights, trusted and true to the cause of creating and protecting trade for the kingdom."

The King frowned. "You, my good knights, are temporarily sore depressed. Your sales are not golden. I knoweth in my heart that you are all good and loyal subjects with great ambitions to grow both the Kingdom's treasury and your own.

"Our competitors, the loathsome kingdom across the river, eateth our lunch. They hitteth on our Buyers. They cheweth us up and spitteth us out. They harass our prices and slash at our flanks with rumor and falsehood. Too often, fortune smiles on these liars and cheats and they hoist their victory pennant over our very own clients"

The sidewalk knights fearfully dropped their gaze; they shuffled in place; they looked at their feet for the King was not to be trifled with when dark of mood and short of cash for palace payroll.

"This must change. You are all goodhearted, loyal, and brave." The street knights raised their eyes to the hem of the King's velvet cloak.

"You are all creative and ambitious. You are the cream of the crop." The knights raised their eyes to the King's shiny breastplate and smiled. Several soft "Yeas" from the group mingled with the King's encouraging words.

"You are superior or you would not labor here among the elite. You are the best street knights in the world...." They raised their eyes to meet the King's hot gaze. "...and you have the best stuff to sell!"

The sidewalk knights began to jump up and down and shout, "Yes! Yes! We are the best! Our stuff is the best!" Their swords rattled.

The King expanded, "You are heaven's own gift to the kingdom!"

The knights nodded and excitedly assured each other of their God-given superiority. They slapped one another on the back and whispered hoarse congratulations to themselves at their good fortune at working for such a great king, "This guy is a great king! So wise!"

The King thrust his clenched fist high into the overcast sky. "Now, go out and win for the King and the Kingdom!"

The knights chanted, "Yes! Yes! Yes! Yes!" They thrust their clenched fists high; if air-punching was good for the King, then it must be good for them, too.

The King flushed, "Do not rest until you recover our lost Buyers across the river! Do not rest until we doubleth our territory! Do not rest until we doubleth our trade! Do not giveth up, unto death!"

"Yes! Yes! Yes! Yes!" the knights chanted.

The King pointed away towards the competition, "Now go! Cross the river. Persuadeth our lost clients to buy our stuff again. Recover our lost territory. Return victorious and we shall all live happily ever after."

With a mighty cheer and their armor a-jangle, the street knights sprinted into the trees through the underbrush to the riverbank where, as their euphoria melted away, they hunkered down together around a small, smoky fire and drank beers into the night. "We soundeth exactly like the knights across the river...." they grumbled. "...the stuff we sell is the same as theirs. The king liveth in a different reality." They then complained bitterly about the competitors who lie at every opportunity.

The King went to bed smiling to himself. He felt powerful for he had set his strategy and marshaled his troops for the hundredth time. "It's good to be the King."[14] he said to himself. Surely this time would be different. Surely, this time he would win.

• •

Appreciation

Iris Herrin is my business- and life-partner; she is the deep keel of my otherwise shallow draft boat. She keeps me on course and away from the rocky shoals of outrageousness (and is the best sales trainer I have ever seen work a room of high-priced and über-educated professionals).

Without her encouragement, participation, contributions, observations, caring (and occasional merciless whippings with a knotted rope), this book would never have been completed. Her ideas, critical thinking and nearly two decades of hand-to-hand combat teaching professionals—lawyers, consultants, engineers, and other highfalutin' fauna—focused us on the common failings that keep those people from living the way they would like to become accustomed.

Her training courses have made people millions.

All of us stand on the shoulders of giants. We have tried to credit the sources of ideas discussed here but in many cases have failed due to the heavily perforated memory of the aging writer. Some of this material has been absorbed by osmosis over a long life from sources long forgotten. If your material has been used here without proper credit, please forgive us; the omission is unintentional, but if you will let us know, we will happily give you credit for your idea in our revised edition.

Ed Crabtree is our patent and trademark attorney. If you are going to sue, talk to him.

Always cool, Rachel Vass "saves me in post" and is a deep resource of humor, patience and technical skill. Great attributes to have in a beautiful daughter.

Our executive-level readers delivered feedback that both encouraged us and hurried us back to rewrite. Thanks to Katherine D'Urso, Bryan Koop, Ka Cotter, Elysia Ragusa, Ivan Preston, John Naisbitt, Howard Camber, Kris Heinzman, Betty Johnson, and Jack Riddle. Their business experience, comments, observations, and edits were invaluable.

We owe everything to our clients, business friends, and champions who invited us into their firms, allowed us to explore ideas, make mistakes, and work from our hearts. They paid us well, educated us, adored Iris, and tolerated Jerry as one would a cranky old uncle. Without our client's forgiveness, we would have never survived. We would never have learned. Thanks for letting us live and learn.

Footnotes

1. DIFFERENTBIZ.COM: a domain name— a close substitute for the real one. This name is owned by the authors specifically to avoid stressful communications with the real firm's lawyers.

2. THAT'S WHAT WE DO: Terrell Hogan, law firm, Jacksonville FL.

3. THEY REGARD HYPE AND OMISSION AS LIES: Kevin J. Clancy and Robert S. Shulman, The Marketing Revolution (New York, HarperBusiness, 1991), p. 48.

4. BENEFITS TO CLIENTS: From website of Duke Corporate Education: http://www.dukece.com. Used by permission.

5. All used by permission of the copyright owners.

6. BUYERS ARE EXPECTED TO AND DO UNDERSTAND THAT THEY ARE NOT ENTITLED TO RELY LITERALLY UPON THE WORDS: Ivan Preston, "A Problem Ignored: Dilution and Negation of Consumer Information by Antifactual Content", Journal of Consumer Affairs, Vol. 36, No. 2, 2002. Ivan Preston, PhD, is the Journal Communications Professor Emeritus of Advertising, University of Wisconsin-Madison.

7. IS CALLED ANTIFACTUAL: Ibid.

8. INFORMATION WHICH JUSTIFIES THE POSITIVE ASSERTION: Ibid.

9. SAP AG

10. The VASS Study. Appendix A.

11. 12% MORE THAN THE COMPETITION FOR
    COMPARABLE PRODUCTS OR SERVICES: Drs. Robert
    Buzzell and Bradley Gale, The PIMS Principles, 1987. Cited
    by Tom Peters, Thriving on Chaos (New York, Knopf, 1987),
    pp. 53, 91.

12. Men go shopping just as men go out fishing or hunting, to see
    how large a fish may be caught with the smallest hook. Henry
    Ward Beecher, 1887.

13. With apologies to Peter Lynch.

14. IT'S GOOD TO BE THE KING. Mel Brooks, History of
    the World: Part I.

Appendix A

VASS Study

Study Objective

To examine the behavior, attitudes, and perceptions of salespeople and sales managers toward their profession.

Study Purpose

To develop effective sales training seminars that respond to those perceptions and behavior and provide practical skills to salespeople.

Study Methodology

Survey of participants in the Vass Executive Sales Training® three-day seminars.

Number of Respondents

3,424 professional salespeople and managers (214 seminars each limited to 16 people).

Length of Study

Ten years, completed April 1998.

Results

Of salespeople,

- 84% believe their products and services are too expensive.

- 93% will volunteer to cut their price without being asked.

- 82% are willing to accept a 90% rejection rate.

- 90% can't tell their business story in a way that involves their Buyer.

- 83% work hard to differentiate themselves but sound identical to their competition.

- 96% never challenge the aphorisms and popular illusions about selling, no matter how illogical.

- 89% of sales hpeople do not understand what business they are really in—from the Buyer's point of view.

- 73% of sales people are unclear why they are in front of the Buyer.

- 77% of sales people refuse to close the transaction when the Buyer is ready.

- 87% will not say "No" to a Buyer.

- 52% never ask for a commitment from the Buyer—even an incremental one—or know how.

- 70% have the facts and statistics to provide proof of their product or service's value yet do not use them.

- 33% who go through traditional sales training, revert to their old way of selling within three weeks of the training program.

- 37% are embarrassed to talk about "real" benefits.

- 48% are satisfied with their current level of performance.

- 70% become uncomfortable when listening to the Buyer explain what they, the Buyer, would like to be sold.

- 86% think that establishing a relationship is how they build trust with the Buyer.

- 98% swear they sell benefits yet, when tested, talk only features.

- 91% ask questions in a way that attacks the Buyer 100% of the time.

- 100% use puffery instead of discussing the quantifiable benefits their products and services offer.

- 75% never establish a sales objective before making a sales call. 85% do not prepare before making a sales call

- 76% are unable to define the Buyer's larger business problems their products and services solve.

- 85% make sales calls with the intention of "presenting" — not to close business.

- 95% are comfortable selling at too low a level.

- 90% are addicted to jargon and features that are confusing and offensive to the Buyer.

- 60% of Buyers react angrily if they are not asked to commit when they are ready to buy.

- 84% of Buyers will readily reveal their problems when asked questions that do not attack their intelligence or emotions.

- 72% of managers believe that selling—the highest paid profession in our culture—can be learned without training.

Notes

VASS excluded participants from seminars lasting less than three days because of the difficulties inherent in obtaining complete and honest responses. VASS will gladly provide any interpretations regarding the above findings. Due to the nature of competition and the study's purpose, the VASS Co. will not provide additional information about the study methodology.

For more information, contact Jerry Vass at 904-461-0452 or e-mail: vass@vass.com. All Rights Reserved © Jerry Vass 1998-2006. Reproduction not allowed without permission.

Recommended Reading for Additional Information

Vass, Jerry, *Soft Selling in a Hard World, (2nd Editon)*, VASS Publishing, 1998

Levitt, Steven D., and Stephen J. Dubner, *Freakonomics*, New York: HarperCollins, 2005.

Lanham, Richard, *Revising Business Prose (4th Edition)*, New York: Longman, 1999.

Inquiries:

VASS Publishing
1093 A1A Beach Boulevard Suite 448
Saint Augustine, FL 32080
904-461-0452